MILLIONAIRE SHOES

WALK A MILLIONAIRE MILE IN 6 SIMPLE STEPS

LEE A. ARNOLD

I'M THE SOLUTION
PUBLISHING

Millionaire Shoes - Walk a Millionaire Mile in 6 Simple Steps
By Lee A. Arnold

Published by I'm The Solution Publishing
ISBN 13: 978-0-9817221-0-8
ISBN 10: 0-9817221-0-5
eBook ISBN: 978-0-9817221-5-3

Book Design by WordCraft

Printed and Digitized in the United States of America

CONTENTS

THE LEE ARNOLD SYSTEM OF REAL ESTATE INVESTING

www.theleearnoldsystem.com

1-800-558-6092

MILLIONAIRE SHOES

$500 OFF ANY UPCOMING SEMINAR

This certificate entitles purchaser $500 off any upcoming Lee Arnold System of Real Estate Seminar

Lee Arnold, CEO of Secured Investment Corp

Authorized by

1 (one) year after purchase

Expires

THE Lee Arnold SYSTEM OF REAL ESTATE INVESTING

Not redeemable for cash - Redemption value not to exceed $500

ACKNOWLEDGMENTS

TO GOD MY creator, who sent his son Jesus Christ, who died on the cross to save me from my sin. Through him I have salvation and the guarantee of an eternity in Heaven. He has shown me that life can be as abundant as I want it to be. If you don't know him personally, I recommend that you make his acquaintance. Then, with His help, be the person He created you to be. He created you for greatness, and it's time to get out there and be great!

To my wife, Jaclyn, who has held me accountable for, and given me the encouragement to complete, my Millionaire goals. You've been my most enthusiastic cheerleader on this journey and none of my accomplishments would have been possible without your constant support. Not only could I never have done it without you, I wouldn't want to. Thank you for giving me the most beautiful children on the planet. Our twin boys, Preston and Harrison, our daughter Aundreya and our son, Harrison Theodore, named for my entrepreneurial grandfather. Living for them and for you, Jaclyn, my life has taken on a meaning I never dreamed possible. I love all of you more than life itself.

To my parents who showed me how to be a good husband, father and a respectable man. I know I complained about slaving away on the farm. But those long, hot summer days, taught me the meaning of an honest day's work and instilled a strong work ethic in me. I'm thankful for those great memories, but I am glad I found an easier way to make money.

To Cherie Constance of WordCraft whose talent and insight helped bring my words to life. Without you this book would have never been completed. Thank you for putting up with my crazy ideas and last minute changes. You actually made the experience enjoyable, and I'm looking forward to working on many more books together. I would recommend you and your service to anyone who wants to write a book. However, you'll be so busy working with me that you won't have time for anyone else. Sorry everybody!

To my workshop participants who continually challenge me to make better products, to create better workshops and achieve higher heights.

To the rest of the world who still believe the earth is flat, that a good education and a good job mean security. As you continue to work at meaningless, dead-end jobs, it makes the accumulation of wealth easier for the rest of us. I hope I can persuade you to stop living a mediocre life of unfulfilled dreams and minimal accomplishment and join me on my journey to abundance.

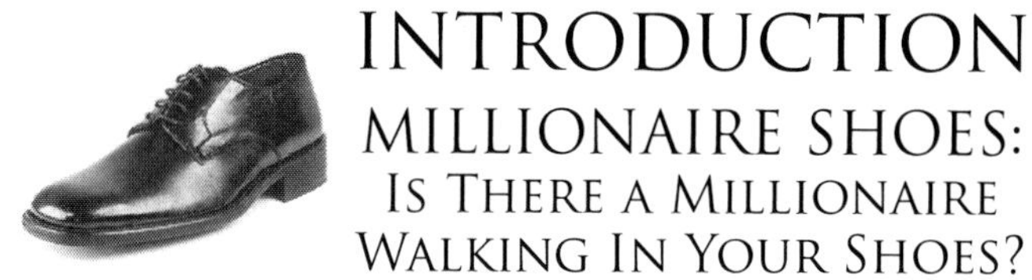

INTRODUCTION

MILLIONAIRE SHOES: Is There a Millionaire Walking In Your Shoes?

Opportunities multiply as they are seized.
- Sun Tzu -

YOU CAN'T UNDERSTAND a man until you've walked a mile in his shoes. But what if walking in his shoes included making a million dollars, or even more? The journey sounds a little more interesting, doesn't it? Is it possible? Of course! If you follow the principles I outline in this book, a million dollars and a successful future can be yours.

I understand that may seem impossible. But that's the first thing this book will help change. You need to be able to believe that it's not only possible, but probable, that you can wear Millionaire Shoes. Because I believed in the probability of my success I was able put on a pair of my own.

Millionaire Shoes is more than just another book about how to obtain wealth. It's an eye-opener to the inner workings of your mind, and how your thoughts influence your actions. You will come to understand why you continue running into financial roadblocks, as well as how to find a way around them. You'll discover that walking like a millionaire is possible if you have the appropriate footwear and a good roadmap.

Solving the Million-Dollar Mystery

> *The man who will use his skill and constructive imagination to see how much he can give for a dollar, instead of how little he can give for a dollar, is bound to succeed. - Henry Ford -*

To be wealthy, or not to be wealthy, that's the question.

Each day moves you closer to, or further away from a wealthy life.

When I say a wealthy life I mean in all aspects of your life, not just your bank account. If you follow the steps in this book and stop dilly-dallying in your so-called comfort-zone, I believe you'll find a pair of Millionaire Shoes just waiting for you.

For many people, making more money is constantly on their minds. Look at Lotto sales? Or game shows -- "Who Wants to Be a Millionaire" and "Deal or No Deal". They're looking to make a 'cool mil' with minimal effort. Nothing wrong with that, but they're going about it ALL WRONG. They're up against obstacles to wealth only Hercules could overcome.

And in the meantime, many play the blame game. Using cop-outs like:

- "I was born to be poor."
- "There isn't enough money for everybody to be rich."
- "Money is the root of all evil."
- "Money isn't everything. It doesn't make the world go around."

Does any of that sound familiar?

Believing any of those notions will undermine your ability to walk in Millionaire Shoes. The sooner you realize that, the sooner you can change direction. Stop meandering around in excuses, and instead, start traveling on the road to riches. Although you might dream the dream, you may think it's just that. A dream. In the meantime, opportunities and blessings continue to pass you by.

But, if you believed that dream could come true, would it?

Quite simply, the answer is, "Yes!"

Thinking about, and believing in, financial opportunity will open doors to a prosperous future. You do have the ability to make your dreams come true. But before tackling the future, you have to learn how to overcome the hurdles of your past and present. Knowing where you've been and where you are now, will allow you to change course to where you want to be tomorrow. You choose how your past affects your future. It can become a lesson and an inspiration -- rungs on a ladder to higher heights and greater success, or it will be like an anchor, holding you back, if it doesn't sink you all together.

You can rise above the person you used to be and become the person you want to be.

Where You Were Yesterday

> *The Past: Our cradle, not our prison; there is danger as well as appeal in its glamour. The past is for inspiration, not imitation, for continuation, not repetition. - Unknown -*

Wearing Millionaire Shoes doesn't begin with a bank transaction or a meeting with a financial counselor -- it begins in your mind. You may be surprised that your formative years are still influencing your current views on money. Past experiences and associations regarding success and money are the foundations on which you are building your financial future.

Think back on your past associations with money.

Did your parents argue about it? Or was it discussed in a negative way like, "Money isn't everything" or "the rich get richer while the poor get poorer?" Do you remember wanting to have more money, then feeling guilty, or being made to feel guilty about that desire? Or do you remember buying things to satisfy immediate desires, like candy, toys, or ice cream? Have you carried those same spending habits into adulthood?

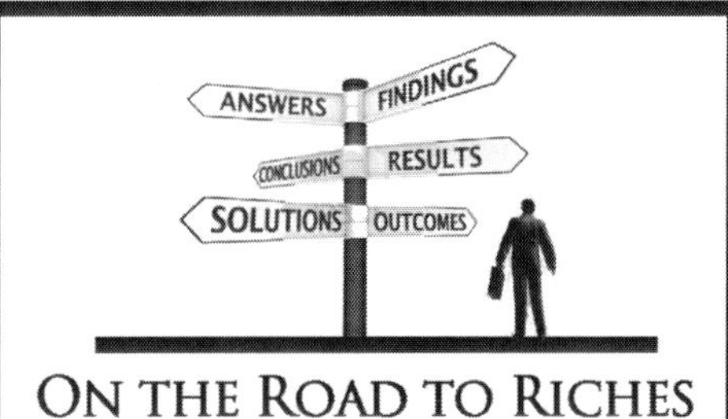

ON THE ROAD TO RICHES

Did you know that the top 1 percent of all wealth-holders in the U.S. own about 44% of the financial assets of the country, mostly in stocks and bonds. The top 10% own about 80% of the financial assets of the nation.

Where do you fall?

If you answered "yes" to any of the above, it's time to build a new relationship with money! Once you do, you can learn to handle your finances properly.

It's okay, and even healthy, to like money, and to respect what it can do for you. But many people have a love/hate relationship with money. Having that kind of relationship with money may be why many people feel the need to get rid of it as soon as they have it. They need it and want it, but money, or the lack of it, always seems to have the upper hand. Finances control the person rather than the person controlling their finances. As if they can't stand too much of a good thing, they have a built-in financial ceiling dictating how much money they should have and how much they can make. And no one can go higher than their own ceiling.

When I was young, one of my first real experiences with money was watching what it could do to or for the people in my life.

My grandfather was my childhood hero. He always seemed to have plenty of cash. Generous with his time and money, he came and went as he pleased, and he never had a boss breathing down his neck.

He owned a large tract of land in the panhandle of northern Idaho where he raised cattle. As a young boy, I went with him to cattle auctions, watching in amazement as the auctioneer's fast-talk made him thousands and thousands of dollars. In addition to raising cattle, he logged his land and sold the timber. It seemed whatever he touched literally turned to gold. He was happy, contented and loved what he did. To me, he represented what money could do for you.

On the other hand, my parents were never what you could consider rich. I'll tell you more about what their feelings about money did to them, in a later chapter, "The Story of an Average Joe."

Because I had questions about money, and how to make lots of it, that my parents and even my grandfather couldn't answer, I had to seek out different mentors.

The business philosopher, Jim Rohn, once said that your financial aptitude and earning capability is determined by the sum total of the five people you spend the most time with. Using that logic, it's no wonder most people who grow up in poverty, continue in that vicious cycle.

To be wealthy you must associate with, and model yourself after, wealthy people. It takes courage to reprogram your thinking, and approach money with a positive outlook. Breaking the mental financial class barrier is perhaps the most important thing you can learn from this book. Once you understand that you are your own jailer, you can escape your self-made prison and create the life you desire.

At your next social gathering, take inventory of the people who are there. How many have or earn substantially more money than you do? If you can't name more than a few, it may be time to make some new friends. You don't have to eliminate people just because they aren't wealthy, but you should make the conscious effort to surround yourself with financial over-achievers.

ROAD TO RICHES EXCERCISE

How do your memories of money affect you today? Answer these questions to see where your emotional money memories lead you.

1. Did your friends or neighbors seem to have more things or advantages than you did?
2. Did your parents argue about money?
3. Did you take money from your parents without them knowing it?
4. What words or phrases were paired with the topic of money? Positive? Or negative?
5. What was the greatest amount of money you saw as a child? How did it make you feel?

Maybe you were jealous of others who had more than you. Jealousy is a negative emotion, and it has a negative effect on our feelings. Parents arguing about finances can make children fearful and anxious about money. That could lead to a person being apprehensive about investing and fearful of risk. Taking money is stealing. Since stealing is wrong, it leads to feeling guilty, and that can tie making money to feelings of guilt. Negative words can create negative associations in our thinking.

Do you see how memories of your past could shape your finances today? By understanding how your memories of money influence you, you will be able to counteract their effects in your current financial dealings. You can stop being a victim to these negative associations and make new, positive memories of money.

Make a photocopy of the following statement, tape it to your bathroom mirror and read it out loud everyday.

YOUR FINANCIAL CHEST

I am not a prisoner of my past.
I am not a product of my present.
I am the hope of the future
I am the solution!

GET OUT OF FINANCIAL PRISON FREE
WWW.THELEEARNOLDSYSTEM.COM

"I AM NOT A PRISONER OF MY PAST. I AM A PRODUCT OF MY PRESENT. I AM THE HOPE OF MY FUTURE! I AM THE SOLUTION!"

Where You Are Today?

Everything is in a state of flux, including the status quo. - Robert Byrne -

When I ask my workshop participants why they work where they do, they often say something like, "To pay the bills." What a boring, unsatisfactory answer. It's a rare case when someone says, "Because I love it!"

Unfortunately, many people are mere workhorses. Maybe they stay in a less than ideal job because they don't believe they can do better. Maybe they think ideas to make money might work for someone else, but not for them. Maybe they think they won't fit in with friends or family if they pursue their dreams of wealth. Maybe they think there is a cap on the number of people who can become wealthy. So, they muddle along in a humdrum existence, complaining to anyone who is stupid enough to listen.

Meanwhile, many self-made millionaires don't actually "work" at all. They happily sink their teeth into their self-made "jobs."

I doubt anyone would wake up one morning and say, "In five years I want to be waiting tables at a coffee shop, making minimum wage plus tips, and supporting a family." But it happens. While no one wishes for an "eke-by" existence, minute-by-minute, hour-by-hour, day-by-day decisions are impacting the future.

Not going to school, not taking a job out of town, or not following through on an entrepreneurial hunch can lead down a path to mediocrity. Many are guilty of trying to live without risk, to stay in their comfort zone. Are you guilty of trying to stay in yours? Don't underestimate the power of fear. The fear of money. Having it. Losing it. Not having enough of it.

Fear can kill any motivation to make more of it. Yet, all aspects of your life teeter on how much money you have and how much you can make. Overcoming fear can tip the financial scales in your favor.

On the Road to Riches

Recently, CareerBuilder.com and Disney Parks took a look at the idea of dream jobs and the people living out their fantasies. According to their survey of over 6,000 workers nation wide, a staggering 84 %, say they aren't in their dream jobs. Many are, in fact, just working to get by, pay the bills, or working to just work.

Why do you work?

~ Because I have to.
~ Because I want to.
~ Because I love to.
~ Because I don't know what else to do?
~ Because I'm scared to pursue my true passion.

What you do next is the most important step in your economic future. You can't change the past but you can focus all your energy on the present and the future. There is no time like now to change course. Stop procrastinating. Put on your Millionaire Shoes and start walking toward your dreams. You'll discover it's actually much more simple than you thought.

Where Do You Want To Be Tomorrow?

Some people want it to happen, some wish it would happen, others make it happen.
- Michael Jordan -

Most people have dreams for the future. Some dream big and some dream small. But no matter the size of your dream, you can only get there if you want it badly enough to work for it. That being the case, wouldn't you rather dream big? Instead of just dreaming to pay off your bills or simply be "comfortable," perhaps it's time to dream of never worrying about money again. The journey to the fulfillment of your dreams, begins in your mind.

Your thoughts influence your feelings.

Your feelings influence your actions.

And you reap the results.

Therefore, if you think rich, ultimately you will find the avenue to take you from poverty and mediocrity to wealth.

A Quick Roadmap To the Goals in this Book

> *Your goals are the road maps that guide you and show you what is possible for your life.*
> *- Les Brown -*

What are your goals? Where do you want them to take you?

- ◊ Maybe you want to overcome the fear of money.
- ◊ Maybe you want to learn to master your emotions, thoughts and actions.
- ◊ Maybe you want to learn the art of having hope, peace and gratitude.
- ◊ Maybe you want to take control of your spending.
- ◊ Maybe you want to be free from credit card debt.
- ◊ Maybe you want to know if an 'Average Joe' can go from rags to riches.
- ◊ Maybe you want to set yourself apart from the crowd.

◊ Maybe you want to have the courage to take financial risks and reap the rewards.

Life doesn't have to be an ongoing struggle; you can experience all the abundance life has to offer. Although each step in this book is specific to one of the goals above, this entire book is designed to help you on your journey to abundance. It will help increase your wealth, but more importantly, it will help enhance your understanding of the greater good in life. And help ignite a fiery passion and the drive to succeed.

You Are the Solution To the Money Mystery

> *If you're not part of the solution, you're part of the problem. - Charles Rosner -*

You, too, can walk in Millionaire Shoes!

You have control over your future and your wealth. Once I learned this, it seemed silly to me that I once believed I had no choice in how I lived and how much money I made. You're either an obstacle or a pathway to your own success.

To walk like a millionaire, you need the right apparel and definitely the right mindset. You'll not only have to change your shoes, but the person wearing those shoes.

You may be wearing the footwear of doubt, fear, envy and defeat. But to wear the shoes of the wealthy, you'll have to shed those clodhoppers, and put on something daring, with style and purpose—your Millionaire Shoes.

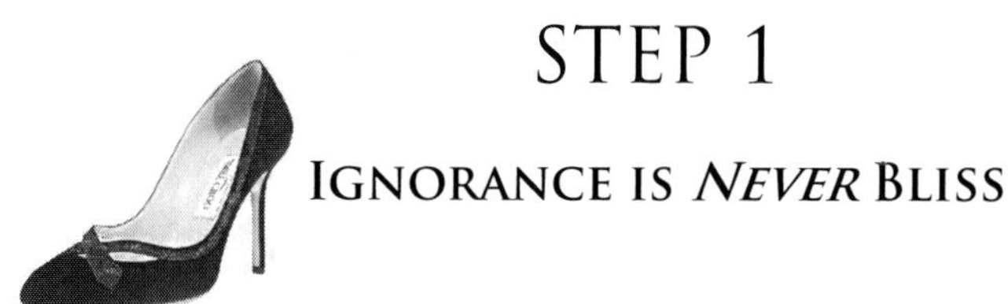

STEP 1

IGNORANCE IS *NEVER* BLISS

The recipe for perpetual ignorance is: Be satisfied with your opinions and content with your knowledge. - Elbert Hubbard -

THE ADVICE AND financial concepts, in this book may be foreign to you. Your first reaction may be to resist them. But please continue reading with an open mind. Often, when someone doesn't understand something, they discard it, thinking it irrelevant or ridiculous. That's a foolhardy approach. Think about it: at one time believing the earth was round was a capital offense. Since the horizon appeared to go on forever, without the ability to measure the planet, it was simply deemed to be flat. And anyone who thought otherwise, and was foolish enough to say so, could literally lose their head.

The same thing can happen with financial concepts. Some people see their financial future stretching out in front of them like the flat earth, without the possibility of change. Thus the adage: "The rich get richer and the poor get poorer." But thankfully (especially if you find yourself on the poor side), it really isn't that rigid.

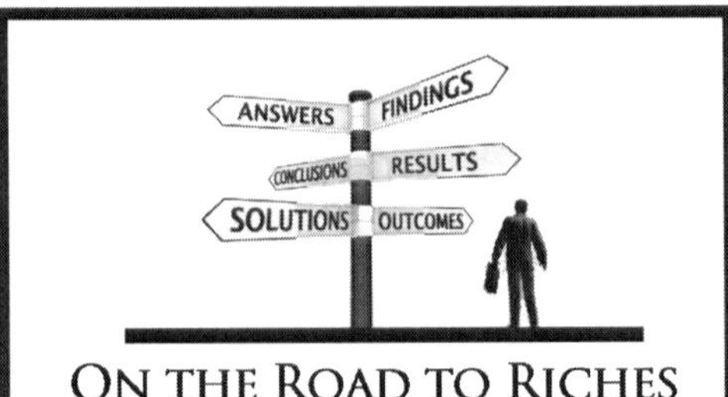

ON THE ROAD TO RICHES

Be an explorer... read, surf the Internet, visit customers, enjoy arts, watch children play... do anything to prevent yourself from becoming a prisoner of your knowledge, experience, and current view of the world.

~ Charles Thompson,
Motivational Speaker

These principles may go against what you've been taught about money and success. They may break barriers in your reasoning and even seem too good to be true. But I hope you'll give them a try. If you do, I can guarantee that the way you perceive your life will take a positive turn.

For many, the road less traveled is the one leading to wealth. Why is that? Because they don't have a road map to direct them on their journey. They get lost along the way, taking detours that lead them backwards rather than forwards. However, if you follow the road signs in this book, with a little gumption, some self-forgiveness and a lot of self-assurance, that road is stretching out in front of you.

Don't let fear cripple you on the journey to pursuing your dreams.

Many people are afraid to "dream big" because they think it "ups the ante" for failure. If they only knew, failure is not the endgame. Yes, it's disappointing. Yes, it's frustrating. But that's not the time to throw in the towel. As long as you stay in the game, and believe you have a fighting chance of winning, there are strategic moves you can make. Understanding your shortcomings and self-made obstacles will not only allow you to succeed where you once failed, but also open new avenues to success.

I believe failure can be defined as, not making any effort to overcome an obstacle, or not trying again and again when you didn't succeed in overcoming it the first time. I'll discuss ways of fighting the failure demon in more detail in Step Three.

Abundant wealth and joy can often be found by departing from the tried and true, and seeking out another road. If you're dissatisfied with the quality of your life, what do you have to lose by trying something new? I believe, no matter what your financial, social, economic, or geographic condition, you can absolutely, 100% become a multi-millionaire. The only difference between those who do and those who don't is determination, vision, and understanding of the truth behind the secret to success—the ability to believe in yourself enough to take the risk.

The Road to Abundance is Paved with Knowledge

> *It is possible to fly without motors, but not without knowledge and skill. -Wilber Wright -*

> *When I was asked, "What is it that I want from the rest of my life?" I remember thinking about how I grew up. I remember thinking that if I could just have the money to always be able to pay the bills or not come home so haggard and broken like my parents, then I will be O.K. I remember Lee saying that if this is what I truly want, then it could be mine…but I could have so much more. I could have abundance, I just needed to expand my knowledge and desire to include more. It was such a simple idea; yet, it changed my way of thinking and life forever. - J. Olson, 32 -*

The first step on the road to abundance is to ask yourself, "What is it that I want for the rest of my life?" Don't let yourself think small. Don't hem yourself in. Don't settle for something just a little bit better than the way you're currently living. If you have little, it's because you dream little. If you want abundance, you'll have to dream big.

Too many people dream small, or not at all. And that's exactly what they get—a "small-fry" reality. Believing they will never have to taste the bitter pill of disappointment or defeat. Yet, if they would strip away the fear, tunnel vision and false sense of security, they would be surprised how much life has to offer.

If you want to wear Millionaire Shoes, you will have to expand your horizon. You may have to gamble. Or push yourself into unfamiliar territory and look further down the road. I'm daring you to dream big. Dream about how you want your life to be. Dream of living in the house you've always wanted. Dream of putting your children through college without debt. Dream of a fun-filled, care-free retirement. Whatever you like.

Now, take those dreams and savor them. What would it be like to wake up in that house. What would it feel like to watch your child graduate from college. You get the idea.

By believing your goals, dreams and desires to be possible, you breathe life into them. And as you do that, they begin coming to life. Keep them alive in your mind's eye, and transform them into living, breathing realities. You can win in this life by the simple act of believing that you can.

Each step in this book brings you closer to achieving your dreams. But as always, the steps to walking in Millionaire Shoes begin with you.

Learning to Master Yourself

> *A man has to learn that he cannot command things, but that he can command himself; that he cannot coerce the wills of others, but that he can mold and master his own will: and things serve him who serves Truth; people seek guidance of him who is master of himself.* - *James Allen* -

Before you can achieve financial freedom, you'll need to be free from your self. So get over yourself! Yes, you heard me, get over yourself! I know that's a bit harsh, but unless you do, you won't be able utilize anything I say.

I'm sure you've heard the phrase, "Actions speak louder than words." Has someone ever told you they would do something for you, then offer a barrage of implausible excuses why they didn't? Most likely you would have a hard time trusting that person again. Yet, we do it to ourselves all the time. Like many people, you may be your own worst enemy. Whether it's relationships, finances, or your health. When I ask students in my workshops if they would trust someone who constantly lies to them, they overwhelmingly answer, "no!"

Then, as they stare at me like they're wasting their money, I ask if they ever tell themselves things like:

- This is my last cigarette.
- No more candy bars.
- I'm going to work out today
- I'm saving part of my paycheck for retirement.

Then I ask if they find themselves retracting their promises. They sheepishly answer, yes. We've all been here, some of us more often than others.

People are amazingly creative at finding ways to rationalize their behavior.

They may use excuses like:

- I'm too stressed to quit smoking.
- A few carbs here and there won't hurt.
- I have the sniffles so I can't work out.
- I can't put money in savings, because (the excuses are numerous; insert your own here).

The most serious problem with this kind of behavior is that we learn to believe that we can't trust our closest ally—ourselves. Because you need to believe in yourself to pursue success, if you can't trust yourself, the pursuit becomes darn-near impossible. Learning to master yourself, and thereby learning to trust yourself, is one of the most important steps you can take, no matter what goals you have for your life.

By keeping the promises you make to yourself, you will learn to trust your self. And a sense of self-confidence begins to grow.

Yes, it's that simple.

Though it may seem simple, many of us find it hard, if not impossible, to keep our self-promises. Why is that? Many times, it's because we're accustomed to failure. Or we fear failure. As I said, I'll talk more about failure and the fear of failure later. But for now, let's work on keeping promises to ourselves by setting some goals.

Once you've achieved something you initially only dreamed of, you will begin to have faith in your abilities. It's like positive feedback. You begin to realize the sky really is the limit, and in fact, you're the master creating your own masterpiece.

ROAD TO RICHES EXCERCISE

When you do this exercise, start small. Maybe just one small promise. The great thing about the promises you make to yourself is that they're usually good for you. I doubt anyone aspires to become fatter, or sicker, or poorer. By making and completing your goals, you will undoubtedly find yourself in a better place.

Smaller Goals:

- "I'm going to walk every other day and take the stairs at work."
- "I'm only going to have dessert once a day and stay away from the candy bowl on the receptionist's desk."
- "I'm going to start taking my lunch to work. I'll lose the extra calories from take-out and save money."

Now, work on your pledges for a week.

We'll assume a week has gone by. Did you try one? How did you do? Were you able to stay focused and keep your promise? If you did, that's great! Good for you!

If you didn't, let's recall the definition of failure. Not trying again and again when you didn't succeed in overcoming the first time. So, I'm rooting for you as you try again. Nothing lost. Go for it.

When you accomplish small self-pledges, how do you feel? Free? Happy? In control? All of the above? Being able to check off the promises you keep will give you a sense of accomplishment and the confidence to take on bigger, more difficult self-pledges.

For example, in my real estate workshops, I ask my students to make a large banner saying, "I will buy one house by ____________" (fill in the blank with a date), and hang the banner somewhere conspicuous, where they'll see it everyday.

Then, I tell them they can't take it down, even if they have guests over. That way they're confronted with their purpose-driven pledge. And they'll have an opportunity to explain it to their friends and family, which will help confirm the goal in their mind and solidify their success.

Since you've had success with smaller goals, it's time to start tackling larger, life-changing goals.

Bigger Goals:

- "This is my last cigarette. Ever.
- "I'm signing up for that financial workshop. Definitely. For sure. I'm going to open myself to opportunity."
- "I'm joining a gym. I'm working out. This spare tire is history."

Stopping the Blame Game

The bad workman blames his tools.
- American Proverb -

Who do you want sitting in the driver's seat of your life? You or someone else?

Most people emphatically reply, "ME!"

Yet, being in the driver's seat is easier said than done. When the going gets rough, we often try to find any other driver than ourselves. If you don't take responsibility for your life, you'll never be able to control its outcome. Although it might seem otherwise, taking responsibility is actually liberating.

No one likes being on the receiving end of blame, but once you can say, "This mess is my own fault. If I work really hard, maybe I can find a way out," then you can breathe a sigh of relief.

Where are you in the blame game? When something goes wrong, how you respond? If you find yourself rationalizing, justifying, or looking around for someone to blame, stop and steer the responsibility back to yourself. Once you can do this on a consistent basis, it will be easier to find a way out of a problem.

Celebrating Achievement in Others

Do you know someone who was born under a lucky star? Everything they touch turns to gold. Every they do seems to succeed. How do you feel about their success? Are you happy for them? Or do you feel envious and think badly of them? Thoughts like, "I could get ahead too if I climbed over people to get there," or "Big whopping deal, another successful millionaire." Thinking like that is wrong, wrong, wrong, wrong, wrong! And worse, it hurts your own ability to succeed. Before you jump to conclusions about how others achieved success, give them credit for their accomplishments.

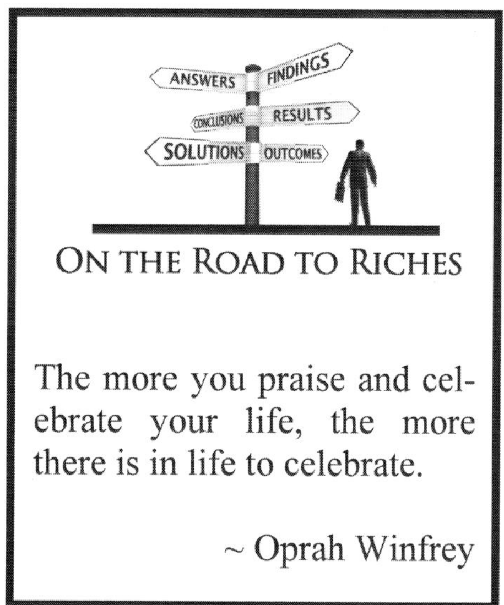

Mediocrity attacks excellence. Pull yourself out of the gutter of mediocrity and celebrate greatness. In yourself and others. Instead of finding fault with their success, think or say something positive, like:

- "Wow, she worked really hard to get where she is. I could learn a lot from her."
- "It took a lot of guts for him to succeed at his business. I want to be like that."
- "Good for him. He deserves to have what he wants because he worked for it."

Saying something positive, rather than something negative, surrounds you with positive energy. It changes where you're coming from emotionally, and that transforms the environment you live in. Until you can admire the attributes of people who have succeeded, it's unlikely that you'll have any crowning achievement of your own.

I coach my workshop attendees to adopt this philosophy: in social settings, think of yourself as the poorest, dumbest person in the room. If you do, everyone there can teach you something. The key, however, is associating with, and modeling yourself after, people who have achieved the level of success you want. This simple thing can help launch you from an "I want" dream, to an "I have" reality.

ROAD TO RICHES EXCERCISE

Think about five people who have more than you do. They could be close associates or famous people. Before you allow your mind to jump to some nasty conclusion on how they must have gotten to this lofty point, give them credit for their success and say something positive about them. Here are a few famous examples with their success stories:

Oprah—Probably the favorite rags to riches story. Although she came from humble roots in Kosclusko, Mississippi, at the tender age of nineteen, she became Nashville's first African American TV correspondent. At thirty-one, she became the first black woman to have her own syndicated talk show. Then she rose above the talk show melodrama, inspiring reading and learning in millions. As one of the richest women in the world she has made it her life's mission to encourage everyone to "live your best life." With her show as a vehicle, she has encouraged people to give to her Angel Network, a charity that supports women, children and families. In 2007 she opened the Oprah Winfrey Leadership Academy for Girls in South Africa, which stimulates high standards of academic achievement and service leadership in young girls.

Steve Jobs—Entrepreneur and inventor, he was best known as the charismatic co-founder of Apple Inc., pioneering the personal computer revolution. Steve was adopted at birth by Paul and Clara Jobs, neither of whom were college graduates. Paul worked as a mechanic and Clara as a payroll clerk. Job's early school career was rocky as he was a practical joker. He went to Reed College in Portland, Oregon. He dropped out, but continued auditing classes, returning soda bottles for food money, and eating free meals at a local Hare Krishna temple. After being hired at Atari Inc., he worked there for several years before leaving to form Apple Computer with his friend Steven Wozniak. He was fired by the Apple board of directors nine years later. He started NeXT Computer, securing funding from Ross Perot. In 1986, he bought Pixar from Disney. When the NeXT operating system was incorporated into The Mac, he went back to Apple, overseeing the iMac, iPod, iPhone and iPad, and iTunes and the Apple retail stores, until illness forced his resignation in 2011. He died shortly thereafter, leaving not only the tech world, but the world at large, grieving.

Mark Cuban—Businessman, investor and philanthropist. Owner of the Dallas Mavericks, Landmark Theaters and Magnolia Pictures. Also, one of the "Sharks" on TV's Shark Tank. Born to a Pennsylvanian working-class family, his father was an automobile upholsterer. Mark's first entrepreneurial venture was selling garbage bags door-to-door to buy a pair of expensive basketball shoes. In high school he held a variety of jobs including bartender, disco dance teacher and party promoter. He also bought and sold collectable stamps. After earning a business degree, he moved to Dallas where he worked as a salesperson at a business software retailer. When his employment was terminated for meeting with a client rather than opening the store, he opened his own company—MicroSolutions. He later sold MicroSolutions to CompuServ, and then formed Broadcast.com, which was acquired by Yahoo!. Cuban then purchased majority share of The Dallas Mavericks and Magnolia Pictures.

Bill Gates—Told his professors that by the age of 30 he would be a millionaire, by 31 he was a billionaire. He attended the private Lakeside School where he discovered his interest in software and began programming computers at age 13. In his junior year of college, Gates left Harvard to devote his energies to Microsoft, a company he had begun in 1975 with his childhood friend Paul Allen. Guided by a belief that the computer would be a valuable tool on every office desktop and in every home, they began developing software for personal computers.

Bill Gates and his wife, Melinda, have endowed a foundation with more than $28.8 billion (as of January 2005) to support philanthropic initiatives in the areas of global health and learning, with the hope that in the 21st century, advances in these critical areas will be available for all people.

Warren Buffet —Talk about someone with the golden touch. As a young boy, Warren wanted to be rich. He purchased his first stock at age 11, and made a five-dollar profit. Since then, Buffett has amassed an enormous fortune from astute investments, particularly through the company Berkshire Hathaway, of which he is the largest shareholder and CEO. With an estimated current net worth of around $52 billion, he is ranked by Forbes as the second richest person in the world, behind Microsoft co-founder Bill Gates.
In June 2006, he made a commitment to give away his fortune to charity, with 83% of it going to the Bill and Melinda Gates Foundation. The donation amounts to approximately $30 billion. Buffet's donation is said to be the largest in U.S. History.

Although these people are successful now, their roads were not initially paved in gold. They started at the bottom and climbed up the mountain to the summit by hard work and faith in their ability to succeed. And I should note, not only have they made a lot of money, in the case of Oprah and Mark Cuban, they have given a lot of money away. Giving will give you the best a wealthy life has to offer.

What You Learn is More Important Than What You Earn

He who knows others is wise. He who knows himself is enlightened. - Lao Tzu -

Though you might have purchased this book to increase your earning power, don't underestimate the power of knowledge. One reason the rich get richer, is that they also get smarter. The value of knowledge far exceeds that of the change jingling in your pocket or the balance of your bank account.

I read a quote the other day that said, "Poor people have big TVs. Rich people have big libraries." I believe that is an accurate statement. I tell my workshop participants, "When you stop learning, you stop earning."

The fact that you are reading this book says something about your potential. When you finish this book, go buy another book about achievement. And another. And another.

And you, too, will be wearing Millionaire Shoes.

STEP 2

IF YOU FOCUS ON DEBT- YOUR SET FOR DEBT

IN ENGLAND DURING the time of Charles Dickens, the words "debt" and "imprisonment" were almost synonymous. But in twenty-first century America—the land of plenty—bankruptcy is no longer a crime, but many people are incarcerated in self-made prisons of debt.

In recent years consumer debt has skyrocketed. The housing bubble burst. Taxpayers bailed-out Wall Street. The unemployment rate soared. Yet consumer debt hovers in the neighborhood of a staggering $11.3 trillion.

Even after the proverbial dam has broken, many people still live well above their means. On average, Americans spend $1.32 for every dollar they earn. They owe for student loans, credit cards, auto loans, lines of credit and mortgages.

So, if you're struggling with debt what should you do? Here are several sure-fire ways to chop away at it.

1. Prioritize debt.
2. Make payments automatic.
3. Live below your means.
4. Buy with money you actually have. Use plastic only for emergencies.

By implementing these strategies, you can break out of debt prison. You can put money into your own bank account or investments, not into your creditor's back pockets.

Hitting Your Head On the Brick Wall of Debt

Small debts are like small shot; they are rattling on every side, and can scarcely be escaped without a wound... - Samuel Johnson -

How many times do you bring up your credit accounts online? How often do you crunch the numbers in your head, on a piece of paper, or on the statement? Is your head aching under the strain?

For many Americans, credit is their financial tool of first choice and last resort. Although they're miserable wrestling with it, they have a hard time taming their spending habits. Struggling to live what they believe is the American dream, they continue "living large" while barely making minimum payments on their credit balances. They have larger houses, more cars and more clothes than they can afford. Everything from groceries to cars can be had with a few clicks and a 16-digit code accompanied by an expiration date. Not to mention school loans, home equity loans and lines of credit.

To live debt free, you will have to wrestle the plastic demon. Simply put, if you can't learn to use credit properly than you should get rid of it. All it takes is willpower and a pair of scissors. Cut up all but one or two of your cards. Take those from your wallet and store them in a safe place. If you don't have the plastic in your wallet, you won't have the temptation. Leave them at home and use them only in an emergency. Groceries, gas, clothes, or paying bills are not emergencies.

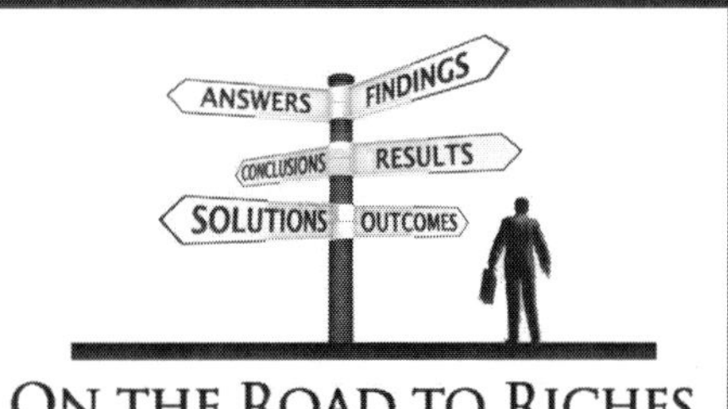

ON THE ROAD TO RICHES

A big part of financial freedom is having your heart and mind free from worry about the what-ifs of life.

~ Suze Orman,
Author of The 9 Steps to Financial Freedom

Prioritize. Many financial experts say it's best to tackle debts one at a time. Pay off the ones with the smallest balances first. Not only will you have a sense of accomplishment, but you can apply what you were paying on the first card to the next one. And so on, until they're all paid off.

Finally, make it automatic. If you have your payments automatically deducted, you won't have the option of spending when you haven't made your credit card payments. Also, making your payments automatic will help eliminate obsessing about debt. It will take the burden of thinking about it all the time. If debt is all you think about, more debt is what you'll get. Making payments automatic will free you to focus on ways to create wealth.

Important Note: Those of you who have attended my live seminars and are involved in advanced coaching and mentoring groups, reading the previous paragraph, you might have thought, "Whoa! Who is this guy? That's not what Lee Arnold teaches."

Those of you who have been to my workshops know that *positive debt accumulation* can help amass wealth. I tell my students that there is bad debt—non-appreciating liabilities, and not-so-bad appreciating investment debt. Meaning, credit card interest on non-income producing purchases like food or clothes, can't be written off, yet the interest continues siphoning money. On the other hand, interest on student loans, mortgages and home equity loans can be used as tax deductions.

Please understand, what I'm teaching in this book are basic principles everyone should follow when taking their first steps toward financial freedom. You need a solid fiscal foundation before you can construct a financial skyscraper.

Building a Good Relationship with Your Money

When you work for money, you find that it is the worst boss you have ever had. When money works for you, it's the best employee you can find. It doesn't take breaks, it doesn't call in sick, and it works 24/7 without calling the labor union to complain about being overworked and underpaid.
- Lee Arnold -

Money is a tool. Used properly it can build wealth. Money can beget more money. But too often, money spent is money never seen again. Here's a look at the spending habits of an average American.

ROAD TO RICHES EXCERCISE

Megan was running late. She pushed the snooze button on her alarm clock one-too-many times. As she was brushing her teeth, she poured cereal for her eight and twelve-year old boys. Without time to eat breakfast herself, she also didn't have time to make lunches for the boys. As she kissed them goodbye, she handed them each a five-dollar bill.

By 7:00 AM, she spent $10.00

At 7:30 Megan jumped in her Ford Explorer and noticed the gas tank bordering on empty. To save time she went to the closest gas station, which was not the cheapest. After filling up the tank, she ran inside to grab a cup of weak coffee and doughnut. The tab at the gas station was $61.55, which she put on her debit card.

By 7:45 AM. $71.55

Megan reached her office at 8:05 a.m. and began working on a design project that was due by the end of the day. She had her work cut out for her. The clients were anxious to see the pamphlet design with the changes they added. At 10:30

Megan's stomach started grumbling and she had a headache. She needed a cup of real coffee and something to tide her over until lunch. She ran to a coffee shop down the street and ordered a grande latte with an extra shot of espresso and a blueberry low-fat muffin. She spent $7.65

10:40 AM, $79.10

After downing the coffee and eating half the muffin, Megan threw the rest away since she was watching her carbs. Back at the office, she worked furiously on her assignment. At noon a coworker suggested lunch at their favorite Chinese restaurant. It was somewhat pricey, but Megan was hungry. And she felt she deserved a reward for working so hard on her project. She splurged on General Tao's Chicken and a glass of white wine. Her part of the tab came to $23.00.

1:15 PM, $102.10

Megan stayed late to finish the pamphlet. At 6:30 PM, she was tired, but relieved that she met the client's deadline. On the way home she stopped and ordered two medium supreme pizzas. They came to $16.99. She gave the take-out her credit card number.

6:45 PM, $119.09

When Megan got home, after dropping the pizzas on the table, her eldest son handed her a permission slip for a field-trip. The cost was $10.00. She gave him all the cash and most of the change she had in her wallet.

7:10 PM, $129.09

At the end of the day, Megan was exhausted. But she stayed up watching "The Late Show." She didn't bother adding up her spending. She didn't even think about. She would do it tomorrow, if she remembered. Or maybe the next day. Or the next . . . or the next . . .

Megan's spending came to a whopping $129.09 that day, with nothing tangible to show for it. If she had tallied it up, she might have thought twice about how she spent her hard-earned money. By getting up earlier, making lunches for her boys and herself, and making her own coffee, she could have saved at least part of the $71.55 she spent by 7:45 AM. Although each purchase, alone, might not have seemed out of line, none were thought-out or planned. She had no respect for money.

Did Megan's day look familiar to you?

While they might not admit it, most people love money. But they don't respect it. They treat it like an abused spouse. They may get what they want from it short-term, but long-term, their relationship with it suffers. And so do they. Whether they are aware of it or not, money is their boss. It dictates what they have, where they live and how they spend their time. Money is the worst boss you'll ever have. But if you respect money and what it can do for you, it will be the best employee you'll ever have. It works 24/7 and never calls in sick. When you put money to work, it works.

Looking at your own spending patterns, does it appear that you don't respect money and what it can do for you? All the little unplanned, unthought-out expenses, added up can become a step, or even a leap, backwards to walking in your Millionaire Shoes.

Think about what you buy. Write down what you spend. If there's any place you can cut, then do it. By planning your spending, and not buying things you don't really need, you'll be surprised how much money you can put toward your financial freedom. By respecting money, you're actually respecting yourself. You'll develop willpower. You'll be able to give yourself a well-earned reward—a sense of accomplishment and self-control.

Having It All, Without Having It All

If we command our wealth, we shall be rich and free. If our wealth commands us, we are poor indeed.
- Edmund Burke -

Too many people spend money they haven't earned, to buy things they don't want, to impress people they don't like. - Will Smith -

A common problem people have with money is feeling that they have to spend it. It's like they can actually feel it burning a hole in their pocket.

Case in point: Lotto winners. If you look at their lives after a decade, many have nothing left to show for their windfall. An unexpected surge of cash surge can befuddle people who have a poverty mind-set. They have the mistaken notion that having lots of "things" equals wealth. Instead of saving or investing their winnings, they buy, buy, buy, or are preyed upon by greedy people.

The same kind of thing can happen to young people who find a great job. They may feel the need to outwardly prove themselves. Not one of my workshops go by that I don't meet a sophisticated looking man or woman, who appear wealthy, yet have little-to-nothing left on their financial bottom-line. Often, even though they are on the brink of bankruptcy, they are leasing fancy cars at a hefty monthly payment, or are weighed down by a leaden mortgage and other debt. They are spenders, not investors. And their extravagant lifestyle sucks potential millions away.

You can have it all without having it all. Many millionaires will tell you that there is wisdom in buying older homes in nice neighborhoods, buying generic brands instead of the hottest new items, and enjoying dinner in your own kitchen.

Look at Warren Buffet, famous for his frugal, unpretentious lifestyle and being among the wealthiest men in the world. He still lives in the same house in the Dundee neighborhood of Omaha, Nebraska that he bought in 1958 for $31,500.

Living Below Your Means

> *A man is rich in proportion to the number of things which he can afford to let alone. - Henry David Thoreau -*

ROAD TO RICHES EXCERCISE

I want you to imagine wealth. What does it look like to you?

- A mansion on a hill?
- A five-car garage stocked with the five most expensive cars in the world?
- Diamonds flashing from neck, ears and fingers?
- Designer clothes and shoes?
- A million dollar yacht?

Many people define wealth in terms of material possessions. According to Gary Shilling's Insight newsletter, How to Make Big Money: 11 Time-Tested Strategies, "lack of income doesn't deter spending." Simply put, the average American spends more money than he or she earns and still has little to show for it.

We envision millionaires as flashy, larger-than-life people who rarely walk among us and definitely don't live among us. Or do they? If you were able to go door to door in your neighborhood and ask, "Are you a millionaire?" You might be surprised who would say, "Yes." Of course I don't advise you to do this.

The idea is that many millionaires are both wealthy and wise. They understand, rather than spending, wealth is best used in other avenues like investment, savings, or real estate—creating more wealth. And the real measure of wealth is net worth. The value of one's assets minus one's liabilities.

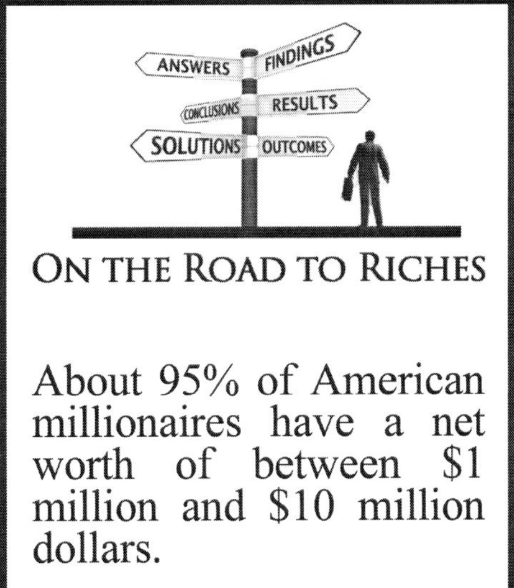

ON THE ROAD TO RICHES

About 95% of American millionaires have a net worth of between $1 million and $10 million dollars.

What's your net worth? That might be a depressing question right now, but it's one worth answering. If you know the answer, you can begin tipping the scale in your favor.

By controlling your spending, you are investing in your value, not devaluing your worth. Once you've crossed the line between living in the red and living in the black, you can enjoy having a wallet again. Instead of being a constant reminder of what you don't have and how much you owe, your wallet can represent your journey toward true wealth in your new Millionaire Shoes.

STEP 3

THE MILLIONAIRE FACTORS: FROM DON'T TO DO

Laugh at yourself, but don't ever aim your doubt at yourself. Be bold. When you embark for strange places, don't leave any of yourself safely on shore. Have the nerve to go into unexplored territory.
- Alan Alda -

I HAVE A framed check for $100,000,000.00 hanging on the wall in my office. It's often a topic of conversation when people first come in. They have to blink once or twice to comprehend all those zeros.
You may wonder, "Is Lee off his rocker? Why hasn't he cashed it?"

The check is made out to me. The catch is I'm the one who wrote it. It's a visual reminder, a representation of a five-year promise I made to myself and my family.

It may seem absurd to have a framed check on my wall without cashing it. The truth is, if I don't believe it can happen, no one else will. I didn't tell you about my objective to brag or pump myself up. I shared it because in so doing, it becomes more real.

Create visual reminders of your promises to yourself, like my $100,000,000.00 check. Put them somewhere conspicuous. Make your goal a subject of conversation. That helps make your promise to yourself become a reality.

Make no mistake, I do believe one day I will cash that check. I won't let a solitary thought enter my mind that cashing the check won't become be a reality. I can guarantee, with absolute certainty, I will accomplish my goal.

You may be wondering how I can make an absolute guarantee on such a bold promise. It's simple. It's an example of what this book is about.

The power of thought. And the ability to believe things into existence.

Harnessing the Power of Goals

Goals can become clouded by the pressing responsibilities of life. Sometimes you have to hang onto a dream like a life preserver in a sea of mundane details.

Instead of fighting for their dreams, many people settle for what they consider "normal." Yet, if you look at great entrepreneurs, inventors, artists and thinkers, you'll see that normal boundaries didn't confine them. Instead, they used whatever creative means they had, and some they didn't, to bring their visions into reality.

These people, who turn their dreams to gold, have one thing in common—they perceive the world as being full of probable successes, rather than full of possible failures. They see opportunity around every corner.

Unfortunately, many people create goals, but don't share them with other people. Sometimes they won't even share them with their own family. They're afraid of being laughed or they, themselves, don't really believe they will accomplish their aspirations.

By not sharing your goals, you miss out on the powerful tools of networking and accountability. Without accountability you don't feel any responsibility to succeed. And without networking, there is no one to help you, should you need it.

The point is simple. Share what you want to accomplish with anyone who will listen. Then encourage them to hold you accountable. Following this simple step can make all the difference between a goal never reached and one far exceeded.

Go ahead. Dream your impossible dream and do what it takes to make it a reality.

The Millionaire Sabotaging Factors

I keep the telephone of my mind open to peace, harmony, health, love and abundance. Then whenever doubt, anxiety, or fear try to call me, they keep getting a busy signal and soon they'll forget my number. - Edith Armstrong -

There are three insidious things that will make putting on your Millionaire Shoes almost impossible.

"Lee, what are they?" you may ask.

They are emotions. Emotions everyone has felt at one time or another.

"Emotions? What do emotions have to do with anything?" I hear you saying.

My answer? Everything.

If you can't control your emotions, it'll be hard to control your finances. The emotions I'm talking about are so powerful, they can stop you in your tracks. They are, Fear, Anxiety, and Anger. And how you react to them, how well you control them, and how much energy you give them can make all the difference between success and failure. If you allow them to creep into your life and give them ground to take root, they will sabotage your ability to believe in yourself. And that will stop you cold.

Sabotaging Factor # 1: Fear of Failure

I always turn to the sports pages first, which records people's accomplishments. The front page has nothing but man's failures. - Earl Warren -

Failure happens all the time. It happens every day in practice. What makes you better is how you react to it. - Mia Hamm -

Fear is a pervasive emotion. News, movies, books and magazines traffic in it. With headlines shouting that unemployment is up, stocks are down, the real estate bubble has burst, and terrorists are living next door, it's no wonder people are on the edge of their seats waiting for the next terrible thing to happen.

Remember Franklin D. Roosevelt's oft repeated quote: "There is nothing to fear but fear itself."

Knowing that newspapers and news stations make money selling bad news, they're the worst places to turn if you're looking for reasons to think positively. Recognize negative influences for what they are. Negative! Don't let them intrude on your drive to achieve your dreams. Turn off the TV. Read books that promote empowerment, and watch movies that leave you feeling good. That will help you control your emotions and stay focused on your goals.

Some people think of fear as an alarm warning of an impending negative outcome, and that it gives them a chance to circle the wagons. The fact is, fear often leads us to inaction rather than action. There are only three small letters difference between do and doubt —'ubt.' When faced with a challenge, try thinking in those terms, and it won't seem so hard to go into action. Take steps of "doing" instead of "doubting."

Take a look at your life. Is your comfort zone lacking in what people normally think of as comfortable? Are you barely living paycheck to paycheck? Do you find yourself looking at the clock at work, wishing the day would end? Do you and your partner argue about finances?

Is that really comfortable?

Not pursuing success for fear of failure isn't comfortable at all, it's cowardly.

Failure happens. But fear of failure is perhaps the #1 reason people don't try. They stay tucked away in their supposed comfort zone, living a tried-and-true existence, avoiding the unknown. Unfortunately, using this approach to life they might not taste failure, but they will never experience the sweet taste of success, either. The possibility of failure is more compelling than the lure of success.

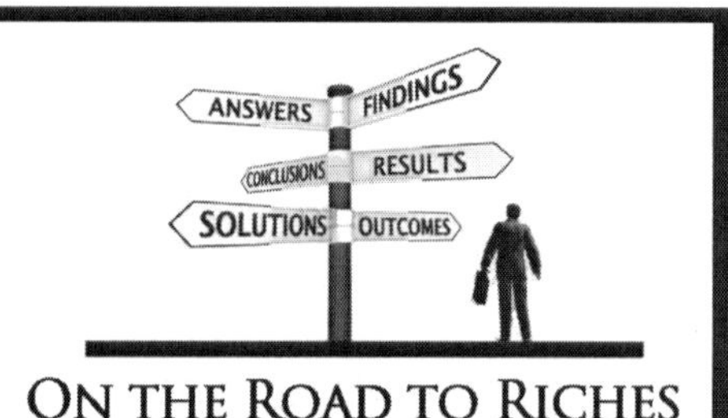

ON THE ROAD TO RICHES

You must sometimes venture into the darkness of the unknown to gain the brightness of success.

I'm amazed that people are so afraid of failure. Usually, it's not about losing family, financial security, or even material possessions.

The adage, "Nothing ventured, nothing gained," sums up the end result of giving in to the fear of failure. Failure is rarely fatal, but it is fatal to a dream to never try. You'll never take the steps to making millions with dread looming over you.

Looking at it another way, failure is often a necessary step on the road to success. Think of it as a steppingstone rather than a setback. In fact it takes experience with failure to truly understand success. The problem is, most people aren't prepared for the possibility of failure. They misunderstand it, they fear it, so when it happens, they're dumbstruck and heartbroken. And that leaves them feeling defeated and less likely to try again.

An underlying reason that many people fear failure is being embarrassed in front of their peers. I find that interesting because the people we usually look to for comfort and solace in trying times are often just as broke and unsuccessful as we are. I've never met a successful person yet, who didn't have several encounters with failure for each one of success.

Did you know most entrepreneurs fail 3.8 times before they actually achieve a goal?

I could bore you with the details of all the stupid things I've tried, and all the money I've lost in bad investments. I often tell people I could've had three masters degrees from Harvard with all the money I've lost. In fact, at a recent Christmas party for my employees and people I do business with, the entrepreneurs in the group began swapping tales of their stupid business moves and investments that went down the drain. In short, we were reminiscing about past failures and what we learned from them.

If you're surrounded by people who say things like, "I told you not to do that. It was a waste of time," or "I told you that wouldn't work," it will be hard for you to take the risks to succeed. You need to be around people who understand that failure can be an important ingredient to success. And that "failures" are often building blocks you can use to build a fortune.

Here are five things to remember about failure:

1.) Failure is not always preventable*:* Once you accept that it can happen no matter how hard you try to prevent it, you can breathe a sigh of relief. You're not the first person this happened to and you won't be the last. Some failures are inevitable. It's best to own up to your part and spend your energy figuring out how to avoid making the same mistakes again, rather than beating yourself up.

2.) Failure is a process*:* There were steps that lead you into it and there are steps that will lead you out. It's rarely: BAM!—you failed and that's the end of it. If you map out the process, you can figure out how to give the story a happier ending next time.

3.) Failure does not make you a failure*:* It doesn't rub off on you, nor do you wear it like a "Scarlet F." In fact, if you look at failure as a building block, it can ignite the fire to try again.

4.) Failure is not final*:* This could be a whole chapter. Failure is never final, and neither is success. Either one can be the starting point to the other. The spiritual teacher, Leo F. Buscaglia once said, "Success often lies just on the other side of failure." If you are at that low ebb, look up—there is light on the horizon.

5.) Failure is Success*:* If you learn from your failures, you have actually achieved success. Failure can be one of the greatest teachers you ever had, if you let it. If not, even if you find the courage to try again, you'll likely fail again in the same way, at the same thing, with the same results. And that being the case, you might as well wear the "Scarlet F."

As I said before, failure happens. Get used to the idea. Then, consciously put away your fear and open yourself up to possibilities. Great men and women failed countless times before they finally succeeded, so give yourself a break. The difference between them and the people who never made it, is that they didn't allow fear of failure to cripple their desire to succeed. It only made them more determined.

Sabotaging Factor # 2: Stranglehold of Stress

> *Over the years your bodies become walking autobiographies, telling friends and strangers alike of the minor and major stresses of your lives. - Marilyn Feruson -*

> *The life of inner peace, being harmonious and without stress, is the easiest type of existence. - Norman Vincent Peale -*

Numerous surveys state that Americans believe they are under more anxiety and stress than they were even a decade ago. A Prevention magazine survey found that seventy-five percent feel they have "great stress" one day a week, with one out of three indicating they feel this way more than twice a week. It seems they're eating, breathing and thinking stress. Anxiety has been linked to many common diseases, and mental and emotional problems as well.

My workshop participants often complain about the stranglehold of stress. They say that they white-knuckle the steering wheel and clench their jaws, more than they whistle along with the radio and enjoy the scenery. Pervasive anxiety will eliminate the ability to see an opportunity, even when it's right in front of you. Why? Anxiety can blind you. It undermines your ability to judge and calculate risk. Instead of seeing the potential for success, you only see the potential for disaster. When you're stressed, all you see is risk.

In the grand scheme of things, each of us can only control a finite number of things. We might as well give the rest up to the powers that be. When I slip into the handcuffs of stress, I remind myself that there's more to life than just me. Instead of letting my focus turn inward, I force myself to look outward. I try to see what others are going through, and think of ways to help them. Removing the handcuffs of stress by changing my focus frees me. I feel like I can breathe again. And I can see the opportunities standing right in front of me.

Although stressful circumstances are part of wearing Millionaire Shoes, it's how you deal the stress that determines your outcome. The following exercises will help keep your wits about you when stress comes knocking at your door.

ROAD TO RICHES EXCERCISE

TAKE THE STRESS TEST

Answer each of these yes/no questions and find out if it's time to take a breather.

1. Do you try to do as much as possible in a short amount of time?
2. Do you become impatient with delays or interruptions?
3. Do you have a hard time asking for and receiving help?
4. Do you spread yourself too thin?
5. Do you do more than one thing at a time?
6. Are you frequently angry or irritable?
7. Do you feel guilty when you relax or do nothing during your leisure time?
8. Do you have little time for your hobbies?
9. Do you find yourself thinking of what you are going to do next before you have the task you are doing done?
10. Are you constantly trying to please others and get praise?

If you answered yes more often than no, try to slow down and implement the six steps to stress-free days.

De-stressing your life is one of the most important steps you can take to open yourself up to wealth. First take the stress test which follows, and then follow my six effective techniques that help you calm down and lessen the daily pressures that blind you to your aspirations and future potential.

1.) Identify the Stressors: Write down the things that are ratcheting up your stress level. Finances. Relationships. Politics. The state of the world. Whatever it is in your life. On a piece of paper, make two columns. One for the things you can control and another for the ones you can't. Obviously, things like the state of the world will go on the "Can't Control" list, while finances and relationships can go on the "Can Control" side. On another piece of paper write down possible solutions for the stressors you can control. Can you compromise with your spouse? Can you begin paying off debt? Any viable solutions you can think of will help lessen the stranglehold of stress.

2.) Breathe: Yes, I know you already do this naturally. But the way you breathe can make a huge difference in your ability to maintain control in a stressful situation. Consciously breathe in for a count of five, hold for a count of two, then breathe out for a count of five. Taking slow, deep breaths will immediately lower your anxiety level. You'll find that within minutes, the anxiety or panic has abated and you're able to handle the situation much better.

3.) Get Organized: This could be another whole chapter. External clutter and disorganization is a manifestation of internal disorganization. Some people claim they function better when their desks or homes are disasters. How often have you had to stop everything because you couldn't find something you needed? Or you realize, as you sift through the debris, that you won't be able to compete a time-sensitive task? Decluttering your home or office will help you maintain focus and work more efficiently. And that will lower your stress level.

4.) Let it Go: Yes, long lines at the grocery store, rush-hour traffic, or kids leaving their toys in the middle of the hallway are annoying, but hardly worth a melt-down. It's important to put irritations into perspective. When something bothers you, rate it on a scale of 1 to 10. Most daily situations are in the range of 1-5. If you find yourself consistently having a #9 reaction to a #2 situation, it's time to rethink how you respond. Reacting appropriately will help you stay in control of your emotions and will also make you a more pleasant person to be around.

5.) Go for a Walk: When your body is tense, you'll have a difficult time focusing. Exercise not only takes your mind off stressors, it also helps boost the brain chemical norepinephrine, which some researchers believe helps curb the effects of stress. Walking supplies a needed rhythm to our bodies, which aids mental clarity and well-being.

6.) This is a Laughing Matter: Have you ever noticed when you're faced with something stressful, a little levity helps defuse potential bombs Laughter is the best medicine for stress. It lowers the stress hormones cortisol and epinephrine. And it's hard to be stressed while you're laughing.

It's important to understand that about ten percent of life is what happens to us, the other ninety percent is how we deal with it. That reminds of a story of a man who came to the table for breakfast with his lovely wife and five year-old daughter. His daughter reached for her orange juice and spilled it on his pants. He jumped up and shouted, "You're five years-old! You should know better!"

The little girl burst into tears, ran to her bedroom and locked the door. By the time the man's wife coaxed the girl out, the girl had missed the bus, and the wife was late for work. Since she didn't have time to drive the girl to school, on her way out the door, his wife informed him he would have to.

By then, he too, was running late. He rushed upstairs, changed his pants, got his daughter ready, then sped off toward her school. Halfway there, a policeman pulled him over and gave him a speeding ticket. When he finally got to work, he was forty-five minutes late. His boss chewed him out, warning that if it happened again he would be fired. Needless to say this guy was not having the best day ever.

Now, let's look at how the events could have been different. He couldn't change the fact that his daughter spilled her juice. If you've been on the planet more than a year, you know things like that happen. However, the spilled juice only represents ten percent of the story. The way he reacted caused the other ninety percent. Had he said something like, "That's okay, honey. Just try to be a more careful. I love you very much." Then he could have gone up stairs, changed his pants and been at work on time. And his wife and daughter would've had a better morning, too.

The lesson is simple. How we respond to what happens is actually more important than what happens. That's an important key in learning how to deal with stressful situations. Before you do or say anything, determine whether it's going to make things better. Or if it's going to make things worse.

By learning to pause long enough to think about how you want to respond, you'll be able to keep your wits about you. That will help you keep your eyes on the prize. And you'll have a lot less stress in your life.

Sabotaging Factor # 3: Anchored to Anger

> *In times of great stress or adversity, it's always best to keep busy, to plow your anger and your energy into something positive.* - Lee Iacocca -

Anger is a powerful emotion.

When harnessed, it can propel you into action. However, more often anger clouds your vision, eliminates your ability to reason and causes you to act inappropriately. To walk in Millionaire Shoes, you cannot allow anger to distract you from your course.

Controlling anger, before it controls you, is imperative to keep you on the path to wealth.

Anger in itself isn't bad. It is powerful. But when it gets the best of you, you're no longer in control. You need to learn a healthy way to express anger.

People generally handle anger in three ways:

Express it.

Suppress it.

Control it.

I believe the third is the most productive way to handle anger. Screaming, yelling, and passive/aggressive responses are hardly Millionaire attributes. While they may intimidate, they rarely win people over to your side of an argument. It's always better to have allies over enemies—especially when you are just getting started on your journey. Therefore, calm down and give yourself a few minutes. This will help you express your feelings in an assertive, but non-aggressive, manner. People will sense that you can control yourself and you mean business. Believe me, you'll gain more respect this way, than if you explode.

Never suppress anger. It's usually worse than blowing up for everyone involved. Often, the anger comes out later in a much more destructive way. You'll either blow up at the drop of a hat over something insignificant that has nothing to with what you were angry about. Or you may hint at how dissatisfied you are in a passive/aggressive way. This kind of behavior is not only harmful to your relationships, it also undermines your own ability to grow and prosper.

Learn to understand what makes you mad. Then learn to control it. Use anger as a tool rather than a crutch. Communicate how you feel without profanity or clarifiers like "always" and "never." Saying something like, "I always told you that would never work, you stupid @#%&!" pronounces doom on the situation, insults the other person and leaves no room for a solution.

How you handle your emotions makes you a candidate to wear Millionaire Shoes – or not.

ROAD TO RICHES EXCERCISE

The Millionaire Freeing Factors

Freedom means the opportunity to be what we never thought we would be. - Daniel J. Boorstin -

The Sabotaging Factors have polar opposites: The Millionaire Freeing Factors, unlike the previous factors, open you to opportunity. By focusing on the positive, you will unshackle yourself from worry, anxiety, and fear, and blossom with hope, peace, and gratitude. When you employ the Millionaire Freeing Factors, you'll be amazed at what the "new you" can attract in the way of blessings and opportunities.

Freeing Factor # 1: Wholeness of Hope

> *Destiny is no matter of chance. It is a matter of choice: It is not a thing to be waited for, it is a thing to be achieved. - William Jennings Bryan -*

What is hope? Think about it a minute.

Some may say that hope is fervent, but meaningless wishful thinking. People who say that have never allowed hope to materialize into something tangible. I think hope is believing something so strongly, that it actually becomes a reality. Without walking in hope, most likely you won't wear Millionaire Shoes.

Hope is a powerful tool. It provides breakthroughs where once there were only breakdowns. When you have hope, your eyes are open, your mind is aware. You're able to perceive opportunities and receive wealth. By having hope for something, you've taken a step away from fear. Fear and hope cannot coexist. It's simply not possible.

When faced with the possibility of failure, hope is a beam of light in the darkening storm. It gives life purpose. It's what keeps you from feeling the bumps in the road and supports you on the journey. And when you're too tired to walk, hope can give you wings.

Write down your hopes. Don't allow the critic in your head to reject any of them. Too often our hopes are subject to analysis, and never given room to flourish. Now close your eyes and imagine those longings realized. Visualizing your hopes gives them even more possibility. If you desire to be a famous artist, see your photographs or paintings hanging in the Guggenheim museum. You're dressed to the nines and circulating through the crowd. You hear murmurings of awe as people are transformed by your genius. Or perhaps you desire to learn to fly. Imagine yourself piloting an airplane over farmlands and mountains—the freedom is exhilarating and the landscape, breathtaking. Or imagine going out the door of your vacation home and walking on the beach with the one you love.

Freeing Factor # 2: Plentitude of Peace

There is no way to peace, peace is the way.
- A.J. Muste -

These days, having peace seems like a pipe dream. Turn on any news source, and the atrocities taking place throughout the world, make it hard to imagine a life of serenity. However, it is possible to live in peace and the good thing is, it's all up to you.

Peace and joy won't simply fall into your lap. I can guarantee it. It takes deliberate action to create them. Make the conscious decision to respect yourself and the people around you. When you do this, peace and happiness come naturally. Making positive statements will help you accomplish this goal. In the morning as you get ready for your day, and at night as you get ready for bed make positive statements like:

"I'm the missing peace in my journey to success."

"I'm happy on purpose. I choose to be happy."

"I'm making myself complete."

"My positive thoughts and actions are opening me to opportunity."

Freeing Factor #3: Greatness of Gratitude

> *Be thankful for what you have; you'll end up having more. If you concentrate on what you don't have, you will never, ever have enough.*
> *- Oprah Winfrey -*

Learning to walk in Millionaire Shoes is not without the potential for frustration and failure. Nothing displaces those negative feelings faster than gratitude.

Research shows that feeling grateful not only boosts emotional well-being, it enhances physical health. Yet, when you're in the thick of a problem, it can be incredibly difficult to feel grateful. It's much easier to fall into a "Why me, I don't deserve this" attitude. But thinking that way obscures your view of the blessings in your life. Feeling grateful, in the midst of, or in spite of, your struggles can help you keep your head above water. It's almost impossible to feel stressed, angry and fearful when you have a grateful heart. If you purposefully recall the real gifts in your life, your mind won't easily wander into the negative.

Keep a gratitude journal. Start writing down both big and small blessings in your life. By focusing on the blessings, you will begin looking at your life with new eyes. Being grateful in both good and bad times, will help you overcome your failings and celebrate your successes.

Being grateful for both good and bad times, allows you to overcome your failings and celebrate your successes.

Keeping Yourself Open to Opportunity

Put yourself in a state of mind where you say to yourself, "Here is an opportunity for you to celebrate like never before, my own power, my own ability to get myself to do whatever is necessary." *- Anthony Robbins -*

ROAD TO RICHES EXCERCISE

Interpret setbacks as steppingstones. Learn to manage stress and control your anger. Reflect on the good things life has given you, rather than the setbacks. As you do this, new avenues to potential millions will open up to you. The potential for abundance is waiting for you around every corner. By plowing your negative emotions into positive purposes, you can reap this abundance. Learn to respect yourself by focusing on hope, peace and gratitude. By purposefully entertaining positive emotions, you open yourself to positive outcomes. The energy you put into focusing on the positive will come back to you ten-fold. And you'll be well on your way to wearing Millionaire Shoes.

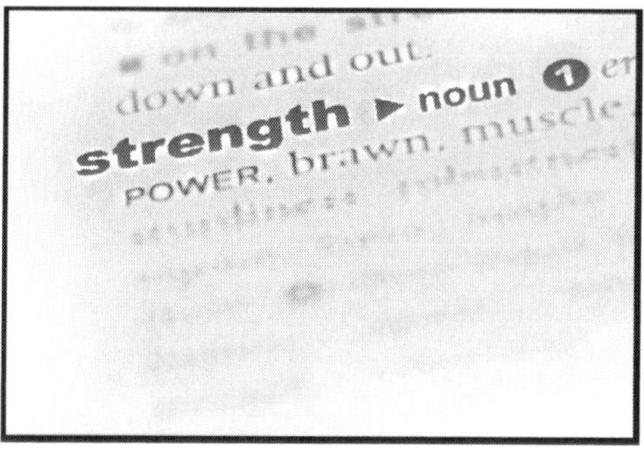

STEP 4

If You Think It & Feel It . . . It Will Come: Incorporating Life Laws Into Your Daily Living

I shall be telling this with a sigh
Somewhere ages and ages hence:
Two roads diverged in a wood, and I--
I took the one less traveled by,
And that has made all the difference.
- Robert Frost -

Life engenders life. Energy creates energy. It is by spending oneself that one becomes rich.
- Sarah Bernhardt -

Poor people do what is easy, which makes their life hard, Rich people do what is hard which makes their life easy. - Unknown -

YOU DO HAVE a purpose. And somewhere inside, you have the drive to put your purpose into action. There powerful life-laws available to give you an edge on creating that reality. This step will show you how to utilize the Law of Attraction.

Have you heard of *The Secret*? The book and DVD swept the nation several years ago. The powerful truth it contained resonated in many people's lives. It taught people how to achieve success, where once they believed they would fail.

While skeptics and critics turned up their noses at what they called "new age mysticism," many claimed this law transformed the way they thought, which changed the way they live.

Law of Attraction: Fact or Flight of Fancy?

> *If one speaks or acts with a cruel mind, misery follows, as the cart follows the horse... If one speaks or acts with a pure mind, happiness follows, as a shadow follows its source. - The Dhammapada -*

The Secret is based on the Law of Attraction, which essentially says, "Like attracts like. You create your life. It is a byproduct of your thinking. Like a magnet, how you think, feel and act pulls correlating experiences into your life."

Common sayings express the idea:

You reap what you sow.

What goes around comes around.

Birds of a feather flock together.

Like the Law of Gravity, the Law of Attraction is always at work. Your life is a physical manifestation of what you think. As you read this book, your thoughts and emotions are pulling their parallel to you. If you're thinking, "This is great. When I finish this book, I'm going to put on my Millionaire Shoes and pretty soon I'll be successful too," your inner-eye will begin looking for ways to make that a reality. On the other hand, if you think, "This is crazy. I can't attract success simply because I want it," you're also right. Your inner-eye will be working to make that a reality.

Have you ever heard of a self-fulfilling prophecy? That's another name for the Law of Attraction. You foretell your own future with thoughts. Whether you're down on your luck or climbing the ladder of success, you're the one pulling the strings. Once you realize that the Law of Attraction is working in your life, you can change what you're attracting.

Now, this is the tricky part. You'll need to weed out not only the negative, defeating thoughts, but the average, mediocre thoughts. And replace them with extraordinary ones.

Let me reiterate, two powerful principles.

A whopping ninety percent of what happens in life is a result of how you respond to what happens. And by believing you can attract what you desire, you can see your desires realized.

For many people, these two notions come as a welcome surprise.

You can change your fortune. This day. This hour. This minute.

This step will show you how.

Do You Manifest Poverty or Plenty?

Decide what you want, decide what you are willing to exchange for it. Establish your priorities and go to work. - H.L. Hunt -

...whatever is true, whatever is noble, whatever is right, whatever is pure, whatever is lovely, whatever is admirable—if anything is excellent or praiseworthy—think about such things.
- Philippians 4:8 -

Whatever you focus on will expand.

It's called manifesting. A manifestation is a four-part process. The natural progression of a manifestation starts with thoughts. It begins by thinking something is possible. That translates into having positive feelings about it. That propels you into acting on it. Then, ultimately achieving the end result.

Each step is imperative. Any misstep along the way can derail the process.

Although the Law of Attraction can be an incredibly freeing law, many people have a hard time putting it to use. They believe that their life happens to them, rather than they are happening to their life. Therefore, they believe they have no control over the past, present or future. This leads to blame, underperformance and victimization. Why try if you can't change course?

Stop complaining about where you are, and get down to business and change it.

The Power of Thinking

Everyone, at one time or another, has heard something like, "If you can't say something nice, don't say anything at all." The same goes for thoughts. Your thoughts are ground zero—the starting point—for the Law of Attraction.

As I said, what you focus on expands. What you think about, read, listen to, and watch will influence the rest of your life. In short, keeping it positive, thinking good, happy thoughts, will produce happy results. Some might ask, "Is it really that simple?" The answer is a resounding, "Yes!" It all starts in the mind. How we think influences how we feel, speak and act and ultimately where we end up. So it's imperative that we start on the right foot. The Road to Riches Exercises in this section show that by tweaking how you think, you can stay focused on success. Keep your thoughts positive, your feelings productive, and your actions progressive and positive energy will come back to you.

The Power of Feeling

Whether you know it or not, what you think about through the day, influences the way you feel. If your thoughts are triggered by broken-record mantras like, "Why me?" or "Everything is so messed up," you'll tend to feel sad, angry, betrayed and defeated. And, thinking this way, you'll be more likely to allow fear to rule your actions, rarely venturing out of your comfort zone. However, if you think something like, "Good things will happen to me," or "I'm going to make it," you'll feel empowered and joyful.

If you understand them, your feelings can be your guide. They're a pretty good indication that you're on the right course, or you've taken a wrong turn. Align your feelings with your goals and everything else will fall into place. If you feel good, at peace and free, most likely you're on the right road. If you feel lost, perhaps you've lost track of the road map for your life.

The Power of Acting

Have you ever heard the phrase, "Actions speak louder than words"? How many times has someone told you they will do something only to later stumble over a barrage of excuses why they didn't do it? Will you have a hard time trusting them again? Actions seal the deal to trust. Once you have thought it and felt it, the only natural thing left to do is to act upon it. Now, this is the tricky part. You need to be able to weed out the weak and unhelpful thoughts and emotions and only act upon the extraordinary and beneficial ones. By doing this, you intentionally and deliberately create what you want.

The Power of Creating

Your thoughts and emotions are the foundation of creation. Everything in your life is connected to how you think. Are you treading water or diving in? It's you who is creating abundance or scarcity in your life.

ROAD TO RICHES EXCERCISE

In the process of "manifesting," an important step is to start checking your speech. Everyone has an inner-voice that either cheers them on or hinders their progress. An inner voice that says, "You can't," or

"You'll make a fool of yourself," or "You'll fail," is using what I call "The Language of Destruction."

How many times have you wanted to do something, but allowed destructive internal language to get the better of you? When you catch this voice trying to speak to you, turn it into the "Language of Can Do."

A few examples:

Language of Destruction	**Language of Do**
• I will never pay off this debt. • I don't want to go into foreclosure. • I'll lose my job. • I don't want to make a fool out of myself. • What if they say "no" then what will I do? • I hope I don't do a bad job.	• One day I will achieve financial freedom. • I am going to own my house one day. • I will be successfully self-employed. • I'm going to do a fabulous job. • What will I do when they say "yes"? • I know I will do a great job.

Notice the statements in each column. Look, for example, at the second and third bullet points in each row. They conjure up entirely opposite imagery. Another example; if you say you're "against war" you're actually using two negative words together – a double negative. On the other hand, if you say you're "for peace," both words are positive and productive. The same goes for the third bullet point in each column.

Although you could argue, in essence, they're saying the same thing, the destructive statement summons up feelings of insecurity, the other gives a sense of hope and empowerment. Success or failure are all in the way you talk to yourself.

I challenge you to change your self-speech. When you catch yourself saying or thinking something negative, tweak it. Turn it into a positive statement. I guarantee, in doing so, you'll begin to feel better emotionally and physically.

What Are You Manifesting?

I have about concluded that wealth is a state of mind, and that anyone can acquire a wealthy state of mind by thinking rich thoughts.
- Andrew Young -

I am more and more convinced that our happiness or unhappiness depends more on the way we meet the events of life than on the nature of those events themselves. - Alexander Humbolt -

Have you ever had a particularly grueling day? Of course you have. We all have. Maybe you woke up thirty minutes late because you forgot to set your alarm. You had a run in your nylons or a hole in your socks. You burned your toast and didn't have time to stop for coffee. Your computer went down at work and you couldn't email documents to your clients. You locked your keys in the car, then got stuck in traffic on the way home. Your favorite show was bumped in lieu of a political speech. Finally, you couldn't go to sleep because the frustrations of your day followed you to bed.

You may say, "C'mon, Lee, how's that my fault? Are you telling me I attracted all that stuff to myself?"

In a way, the answer is yes.

The issue isn't if you have the gift of manifestation—everyone has it. The issue is whether you're manifesting positively or negatively. Like the law of gravity, the Law of Attraction, is not subjective. It doesn't prefer one type of energy over another. The type of energy you put out will come back, either to bless or haunt you. The Law of Attraction doesn't decide, you do. So, the real question is, "What are you manifesting in your life?" Do you want to change it?

Notice the different types of words used in each column. Look, for example, at the second and third bullet points in each row. Notice that on first glance they seem to be saying the same thing. Yet, if you dissect the words, they conjure up entirely opposite imagery.

Another example is the words War and Peace, which are diametrically opposed. Although you are saying you are "against war" you're saying two negative words together. On the other hand, if you say you are "for peace" you are uttering language that is positive and productive. The same goes for the third bullet point in each column. Although you are basically saying the same thing, the first statement summons up feelings of insecurity and fear, while the second one fills you with hope and empowerment. It is all in the way you talk to yourself and others.

> *Every person has the power to make others happy.*
> *Some do it simply by entering a room—others by leaving the room.*
> *Some individuals leave trails of gloom;*
> *others, trails of joy.*
> *Some leave trails of hate and bitterness;*
> *others, trails of love and harmony.*
> *Some leave trails of cynicism and pessimism;*
> *others trails of faith and optimism.*
> *Some leave trails of criticism and resignation;*
> *others trails of gratitude and hope.*
> *What kind of trails do you leave?"*
>
> *~ William Arthur Ward*
> *American dedicated scholar,*
> *author, editor, pastor and teacher*

I challenge you to change your self-speak. When you catch yourself saying something that is at its root a negative statement, tweak it. Turn it into a positive sentence. I guarantee that in doing so, you will feel better both emotionally and physically. Everything is connected to how you think about your various situations—are you treading water or diving in? Your thoughts will determine this.

ROAD TO RICHES EXCERCISE

Creating Visualization Reminders

Sometimes you need a nudge, here and there, to keep you on the right track. I've found that using visual cues is a powerful way to keep my eyes on the prize. The act of putting your desires on paper and keeping it where you will see it, will help you stay focused and confident on your journey.

Goal Clarifying

As I said, what you focus on expands. It helps if you spell out what it is that you're seeking. If you put effort into making your goals clear, the universe will begin working with you. Writing your goals down, then repeating them in your mind and saying them out loud, sets their manifestation in motion.

It's important to note that clarifying goals is not writing down things you don't want. Nor should you concentrate on what you haven't accomplished. Once you focus on the can'ts, 'won'ts and haven'ts you're undermining your success by allowing negative thoughts to invade your goals.

Goal Symbols and Collages

When you were little, did you ever sit down with a toy catalogue, point to something and say, "I want that!" Just by looking at the picture, you felt the excitement of playing with that new toy.

Even as adults, we have the desire for things. And like a child looking at pictures of something wished for and feeling the excitement of having it, we can use the same mechanism to achieve our goals. I'm not advocating materialism, but the fulfillment of honest-to-goodness goals.

For visually oriented people, a goal collage is an effective tool. Clip pictures from magazines that represent what you want to acquire or accomplish. Maybe you want to redo your landscaping. Find pictures similar to what you want to do with your yard. Put them on your refrigerator, or somewhere you'll see them. Maybe you want to build your dream house. Create a collage of pictures that resemble what you want your dream home to look like. If you want to start a business, find something that symbolizes this for you—like pictures of houses or "sold"" signs if you want to be a realtor.

Whenever you look at your collage, you'll be reminded of what you want to accomplish.

Mental Message Massages

Placing inspirational and motivational messages around your home and office will help you stay purposeful and positive. There's more than enough negative messaging in the world. Why not offset it with something positive?

The five inspirational statements below helped me stay focused on my personal aspirations. Write or type these statements, or some of your own, then hang them in a conspicuous place. When you're feeling discouraged, seeing something positive will raise your spirits and help buoy you up. I guarantee it.

> *Do not pray for easy lives. Pray to be stronger men. Do not pray for tasks equal to your powers. Pray for powers equal to your tasks. Then the doing of your work shall be no miracle, but you shall be the miracle. - Phillips Brooks -*

Don't waste yourself in rejection, nor bark against the bad, but chant the beauty of the good.
- Ralph Waldo Emerson -

The embodiment of the information you choose to accept and act upon. To change your circumstances you need to change your thinking and subsequent actions. - Adlin Sinclair -

Your time is limited, so don't waste it living someone else's life. Don't be trapped by dogma - which is living with the results of other people's thinking. Don't let the noise of other's opinions drown out your own inner voice. And most important, have the courage to follow your heart and intuition. They somehow already know what you truly want to become. Everything else is secondary.
- Steve Jobs -

If your actions inspire others to dream more, learn more, do more and become more, you are a leader.
- John Quincy Adams -

Choose Your Own Adventure

Your life is the sum result of all the choices you make, both consciously and unconsciously. If you can control the process of choosing, you can take control of all aspects of your life. You can find the freedom that comes from being in charge of yourself.
- Robert F. Bennett -

Did you read the "Choose Your Own Adventure" books when you were young? At the bottom of a page, at a crucial point in the story, you were given two options and correlating page numbers for each option. One led to choices with an eventual positive outcome, while the other led to peril, or worse, death. The great thing was, you could try both options to see where either choice would take you.

Life is the same way. But in real life, it's not as easy as flipping back a few pages to make a different choice. The choices we make about how we feel, believe and act, will either bring us joy, contentment, opportunity and success, or lead us down a path of discouragement and despair. Knowing that you choose your own future, it makes sense to choose a positive outcome.

The law of attraction, gives you this opportunity, whether you utilize it or not. You're not predestined to succeed or doomed to fail. There aren't any lucky horoscopes or star signs, but you're not naturally unlucky either. You're what you've made of yourself. Who you are now is not who you have to be in the future. Starting now, by utilizing the information in this step, you can wear Millionaire shoes.

Think of what an amazing adventure you can have!

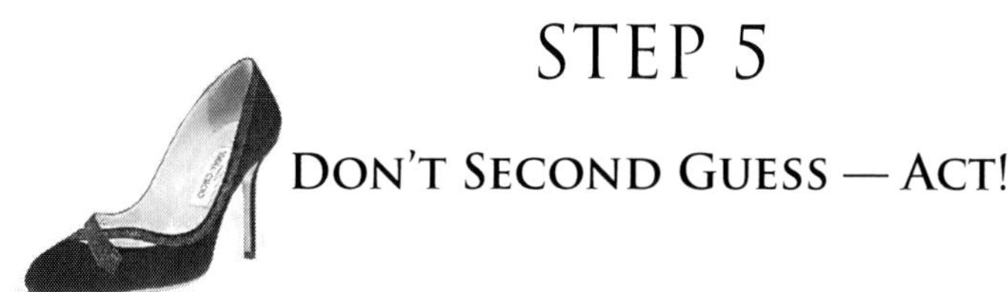

STEP 5

DON'T SECOND GUESS — ACT!

It's not because things are difficult that we dare not venture. It's because we dare not venture that they are difficult. - Seneca -

SOMEONE OUT THERE is making money, even in a down market. There will always be people who find innovative ways to create wealth. You just need to learn how to be one of them.

The mind is a powerful tool. But too often it's wasted on "what-ifs" of life. Some people are so gifted at imagining "what ifs," they concoct imaginary scenarios down to the last detail. Thinking about what might have happened if only they had done one thing or another differently.

When asked about their "what-ifs," the people attending my real estate workshops often say things like:

> "What will people think if I quit my job to work for myself?"
> "What if I can't support my family?"
> "What if my spouse won't go along with me on this venture?"
> "What if I can't pay my bills and my house goes into foreclosure?"
> "What if everything I invest in my company goes up in smoke?"
> "What if, what if, what if..."

In their minds, before they've even started, they've already lost their homes, their spouses, their businesses, and their standing in the community. It's no wonder they don't have the stomach to follow their dreams—they've already imagined failure in vivid detail. You see how easily the imagination can spiral out of control. And to make matters worse, while you're 'what-ifing' negative possibilities, you're not living in the now.

You can't win if you don't believe you can complete the race. Or, if you don't even believe there is a race. But you can win by acting on the belief that you can. Don't let your worries be a stop sign on your road to riches. Instead, let them be a conduit for growth. If you're feeling uncomfortable, it's likely you're growing, and going in the right direction. Remember, remaining in your comfort zone keeps you from reaching for more lucrative horizons.

> *Courage is not the absence of fear, but rather the judgment that something else is more important than fear. - Ambrose Redmoon -*

> *Life shrinks or expands in proportion to one's courage. - Anais Nin -*

Poor vs. Plenty: A Lesson in Be-Attitudes

The attitudes of many millionaires go deeper than their pockets. They are often go-getters and self-starters, who prove that having a positive outlook creates a positive income. What are the characteristics that set the wealthy apart? And, most importantly, can those traits be learned?

Happily, the answer is yes!

So, what's the bird's eye view? What characteristics are common to successful people? And what attributes are commonly found in people who fail? By practicing the qualities of success, they will become second nature. And when you imitate success, you'll soon find that the imitation becomes genuine.

Attitudes That Attract Poverty

1. *Complaining about work.*
2. *Believing in others more than yourself.*
3. *Being disorganized.*
4. *Being wishy-washy.*
5. *Letting problems fester instead of tackling them.*
6. *Allowing negativity to take root.*
7. *Visualizing the worst-case scenario.*
8. *Fearing failure more than hoping for success.*

Attitudes That Attract Plenty

1. *Giving to those less fortunate, both time and money.*
2. *Not shirking hard work.*
3. *Believing in yourself.*
4. *Being prepared.*
5. *Being decisive and having clarity of direction.*
6. *Taking immediate action to solve problems.*
7. *Thinking positively.*
8. *Being grateful.*
9. *Visualizing success.*
10. *Not allowing fear to overwhelm your desires.*

Courage=Wealth

Be faithful to that which exists nowhere but in yourself—and thus make yourself indispensable.
- Andre Gide -

Webster's dictionary defines courage as "mental or moral strength to venture, persevere, and withstand danger, fear, or difficulty."

Self-made millionaires epitomize this definition. They understand the wisdom and strength that comes from being bold. They take financial risks – owning their own companies and investing. They understand that sometimes things work, and sometimes they don't. And that when it works, it really pays off.

If you begin to see risk differently, you'll see it as a means to an end. The benefits of financial freedom outweigh the risks involved in getting there.

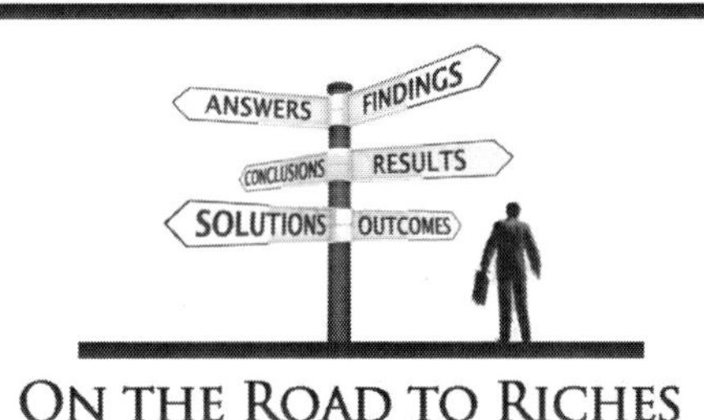

ON THE ROAD TO RICHES

I never start a road trip without a map and I've never conducted business without a map either. If you're really going to be successful you have to know at all times, regardless of where you are, where you are going. To attempt to do anything without a direction is nothing more than turning circles in the back yard.

Who do you trust more than yourself? Most people's immediate answer: "No One!" Yet, many of us allow circumstances and other people to determine our destiny. Stop second-guessing yourself. Either you're in the driver's seat, or someone else is. Take steps toward a positive financial future. Take charge, take action and take control. If you don't, someone else will and that's usually not in your best interest.

In this Step, you'll learn how to calculate risk versus reward and avoid getting tangled up in the what-ifs of life.

Miscalculating Risk

Man cannot discover new oceans unless he has the courage to lose sight of the shore. - Andre Gide -

Gambling vs. Risk

Some people look at millionaires as being lucky. They have a hard time separating the idea of taking a financial risk from gambling. Self-made millionaires are lucky in the respect that they usually work hard and believe in themselves. As I've said, financial freedom is not a matter of luck, but a matter of will, hard work and discipline. In fact, most millionaires usually won't set foot in a casino unless they're going to a business meeting, a trade show, or they own it. They respect money too much to throw it away on a crapshoot.

I'm not suggesting you should gamble with your finances, either. But like attracts like, so if you believe you'll be lucky in business, most likely you will be.

If there's a will, there's always a way to turn life's 'what-ifs' into 'what-wills.'

The What-Ifs	The What-Wills
1. What if I fail?	1. I will succeed.
2. What if I can't be self-employed?	2. I will have a successful business.
3. What will happen if no one will finance me?	3. I will find an excellent team.
4. What if I lose all my money in the stock market?	4. I will research and find stocks that work the best for me and will provide the best return.
5. What if I can't sell the flip properties I bought?	5. There are enough buyers out there that I will always find one.
6. What if I will never be happy?	6. I will find happiness within myself.

So, what does financial risk look like to you?

When I ask my workshop participants this question, I receive a slew of different answers. Some of the most common are:

- Investing in the stock market.
- Being self-employed.
- Buying real estate.
- Not finishing college.

I have responses for each of these supposed financial risks.

The Stock Market

Common wisdom tells us the stock market isn't for the faint of heart. The moody fluctuations of the market can make even seasoned investors queasy. Fortunes can be made or lost in moments. It takes courage to put your hard- dollars into the hands of corporate America. It takes even more courage to hang onto your investments in an environment of panic. However, it's those who do that usually end up making a profit. The key is, not reacting to a drop here or there in the market, but having the discipline to stay the course. I've known people who made millions while earning a blue-collar income by mastering the stock market. They had the courage to take modest earnings and turn them into mega-earnings by investing.

I encourage you to become a student of the stock market. Read about it, study corporations and their investment options. Even if your eyes glaze over at the mere mention of spread sheets and numbers, stocks can still be a lucrative option. And it's considered passive income, since there is no actual labor involved in making a profit.

Self-Employment

Some people can't imagine living without a regular paycheck. Like a life preserver, they believe that paycheck will keep them afloat in a sea of financial insecurity. They believe, if they have a job, they won't have to worry about where their money is coming from. The paycheck, insurance and other benefits, give them a feeling of security.

Although a job can offer some security, you're still just an employee. Minimum and maximum effort often produce the same result—a regular paycheck. As long as the company stays in the black, assuming you're doing a reasonably good job, you stay on the payroll. But what happens when they dip into the red? Workers are often first to go when a company needs to cut costs.

Being self-employed can be rewarding enough to balance the risk of taking the plunge. It has been for me. If a former grocery store bagboy, college dropout, can become a multi-millionaire, then there's no reason you can't too. I've never looked back with longing about working for someone else.

Self-made millionaires take risks. It comes with the package. Although it can be dicey to work for yourself, there are just as many risks working for someone else. Owners usually work harder than employees to make a company succeed. And they believe in what they do.

You shouldn't go into a business venture if you think it might not work. If failure is an option before you've even started, then I can almost guarantee you'll fail. But if failure's not an option, it's not even on the radar screen, and there's nothing anyone can do to stop you, then I can almost guarantee that you'll succeed.

Home and Real Estate Ownership

Being a successful real estate investor, I'm always surprised that people are afraid of owning property. In my opinion, buying and selling real estate is the easiest way to make a large amount of money in a short amount of time. Even home ownership usually makes more sense than renting. At least the money is going toward owning something you most likely love.

Often people don't think seriously about owning real estate because they don't have a large salary, good credit, or a big down payment. The reality is that in the real estate world, money is lent on the property, not to people. In the simplest sense, that means anyone can do it. If the property is a good deal, you may have to look around, but you'll find someone to fund it.

Don't buy into some people's negative view of investing in real estate. If you're interested in real estate as an investment, I invite you to come to one of my workshops. You'll find locations and dates for upcoming workshops at **www.theleearnoldsystem.com.** The coupon at the front of this book is good for $500 off any upcoming seminar. I cover real estate investment in more depth. You'll learn what to look for in investment properties, how to approach sellers, how to negotiate a sale and how to sell the property for a higher price.

College Education

Everything in life is accompanied by a measure of risk. Whether you decide to finish college or not. Many believe not having a degree is financial suicide. But in many ways a diploma is just a piece of paper. You're the vehicle for a formal education's use, misuse, or disuse. A college degree is only what you make of it. For some, it opens doors. For others, it stifles progress.

I realized after my first semester, a college degree wouldn't help me advance in my chosen field—real estate. I couldn't acquire the experience I needed sitting in a classroom. I had to attend the "University of Life." I graduated with a Ph.D. in rapid wealth creation.

Now, I don't advocate that everyone skip out on school. Some professions, like law, medicine, science, require a degree. I'm not excited about having a college drop-out operate on me or represent me in court. Yet, many self-made millionaires didn't attend college. It wasn't education, but drive and courage, that determined their success.

Are You a Problem Person or a Solution Person?

If you listen to your fears, you will die never knowing what a great person you might have been.
- Robert H. Schuller -

Problems become insurmountable only when you aren't willing to work to create a solution. Many people procrastinate because they don't want to deal with a negative issue. But the sooner you start dealing with it, the sooner you can put it to bed.

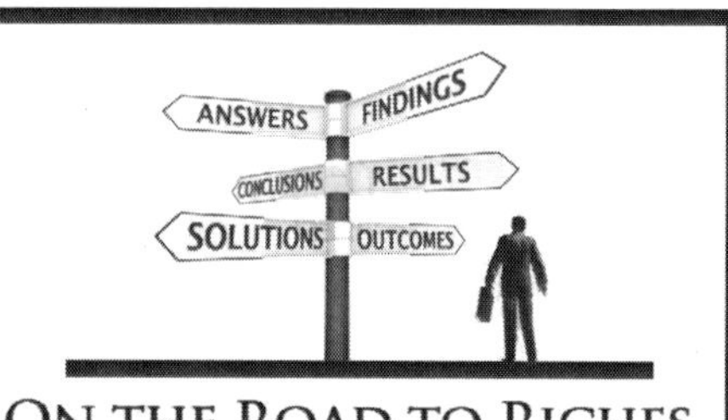

ON THE ROAD TO RICHES

The person who risks nothing, does nothing, has nothing, is nothing, and becomes nothing. He may avoid suffering and sorrow, but he simply cannot learn and feel and change and grow and love and live.

~ Leo F. Buscaglia
American Guru

When it comes to solving problems, your mind can be your biggest stumbling block. It can make the proverbial mountain out of a molehill. For example, thinking, "I'll never get out from under this debt." When you extrapolate the true meaning, this sentence is a double negative. By using never and debt in the same sentence, you're mentally dooming yourself to a self-perpetuated financial black hole.

To go from being a problem person to a solution person, you need to eliminate certain thoughts from your mind and certain words from your vocabulary.

Words like: never, won't, what if, and can't. They're all self-defeating. You're talking yourself out of a solution and perpetuating a problem. When you catch yourself saying or thinking sentences containing these self-negations, stop and change the statement to a more positive one.

In addition, there is one word that makes my skin crawl more than maybe any other. I'm referring to: TRY. When it's used like an escape hatch, it's insincere and allows for failure. Then it looks back and makes perhaps the dumbest statement in the English language: "Well, at least I tried."

When you become aware of the way people use the word "try" you'll hear it all the time. For example, I had plans to meet a friend for lunch. I asked what time he'd be there. His comment: "I'll try to be there by noon." What did he mean by that? Will he be there at noon or won't he? I knew exactly what he meant. He meant he probably wasn't going to be there on time. And he wasn't. At least he could have said at the onset that he had a conflict or whatever the issue was.

In my opinion, the word try used that way, is a bunch of hooey.

You might say, "But Lee, I'm just trying to get out of my comfort zone. How can I do that if I don't try?" The difference is allowing for failure before you've even tried. There are actually only two outcomes to any venture. Either you will succeed or you will fail. A stronger, more positive way to say it is, "I'm going to work at getting out of my comfort zone, and I'm going keep working at it until I'm free."

If you're a person who tries everything, chances are, you often fail. You're either going to give everything you have within you to do something or you aren't. Be specific about what you intend to accomplish. And don't give the impression, even to yourself, that you'll try to do something if you don't intend to do everything in your power to accomplish it.

Be decisive. None of the successful people I know are wishy-washy about what they are and are not going to do. There is no faster way to get where you're going than to stop trying and start doing.

ROAD TO RICHES EXCERCISE

Solution Clustering

It's called problem and solution clustering. You write a problem in the middle of the page and circle it. From that point, you branch off into possible solutions. From those solutions, you make more lines of possible issues or benefits regarding each solution.

Action vs. Reaction

> *High achievers spot rich opportunities swiftly, make big decisions quickly and move into action immediately. Follow these principles and you can make your dreams come true. - Robert H. Schuller -*

> *Inaction breeds doubt and fear. Action breeds confidence and courage. If you want to conquer fear, do not sit home and think about it. Go out and get busy. -Dale Carnegie -*

Oprah Winfrey once featured a professor of computer science from Carnegie Mellon University on her show. I'm not a close follower of computer science; however, Randy Pausch left a lasting impression on me. I remember him saying, "Experience is what you get when you didn't get what you wanted."

He should know. He was diagnosed with terminal cancer. But in light of that, or because of that, he wrote an eloquent final lecture to his students. It was a kind of battle cry to live life well, to never waste a moment, and to stop wallowing in self-pity.

What really got to me was, even while faced with eminent mortality, he embodied courage, optimism, and faith in mankind. He was the personification of the statement, "Life is what you make it."

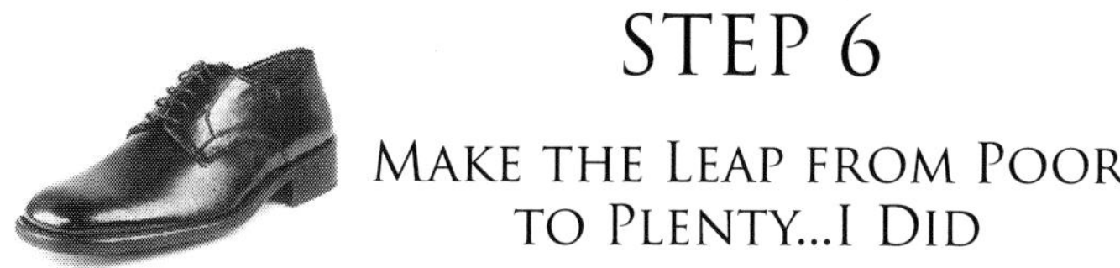

STEP 6

Make the Leap from Poor to Plenty...I Did

If you want to make good use of your time, you've got to know what's most important and then give it all you've got. - Lee Iacocca -

YOU'RE ONLY A few short steps away from success. They're relatively straightforward—think, act, receive. But many people stop short. Sure, they imagine the castle in the sky. But they never find the vehicle to take them there, or the gauge on their meter motivation and courage is always on empty.

If you don't believe the castle in the sky is real, then for you it isn't. If you don't really believe you'll be wealthy one day, then you absolutely won't. Even if a rich relative dies and leaves the castle to you, or you win it in a lottery, most likely you'll eventually lose it because you never actually saw yourself living in it.

Until you have the mentality of a rich man or woman, you won't be one.

This reminds me of a story about a man who was on a journey. He came across another man sitting beside the road near a town. The first man asked, "What are the people like in the next town?"

The other fellow answered with a question: "What were the people like in the town you just came from?"

The traveling man began a litany of complaints. "They are rude, liars, and manipulators. They were mean and said awful things about me. I hate all of them."

The other man shook his head and replied, "Oh, that's too bad, the people in the next town are exactly the same as the people in the town you just left."

The first man sighed sadly and continued on his journey.

Not too long after, another man approached the fellow sitting beside the road. He, too, asked what the people were like in the next town. The fellow again responded with the question, "What were the people like in the town you just left?"

"Oh, they were great. I had nice, helpful neighbors and wonderful, thoughtful friends. I loved them and I hated to leave."

The fellow smiled and responded saying, "You're in luck. You'll find that the people in the next town are exactly the same as the people you left."

The point of this story is, your life is what you make it.

It's not money that makes you happy, but happiness will prepare you to have money. As "The Law of Attraction" teaches, think success, act successfully and be successful. Your life is yours to dictate and control. If life is great, it's because you believe it's great. If life is bad, it's because you believe it's bad. It really is that simple. It's your call and your choice, so make sure you choose wisely.

> *If you want to make good use of your time, you've got to know what's most important and then give it all you've got. - Lee Iacocca -*

Fear stagnates progress, while courage stimulates growth. Many times when people don't see immediate results from a new endeavor, they become doubtful, disappointed and give up. Courage to stick with it will break the mediocrity mold. It's the ingredient that will take a vision and make it a reality. Without courage, you're just like a guy pushing a broom for a living and wishing for a better day.

ROAD TO RICHES EXCERCISE

Breaking the Mediocrity Mold With Four Simple Cracks

First Crack: Investing in Yourself

It takes courage to believe in yourself. You may have a hard time promoting yourself or your product. But that's what you'll have to do to wear those Millionaire Shoes.

There are several reasons why people have a hard time selling themselves. First, they may associate selling with people who call them during dinner and hard-sell them something they don't want. Second, they may have felt the bitterness of rejection. And third, they may worry about coming across as a braggart. They've been taught it's not polite to pat yourself on the back.

My response is this: First, the salesperson controls the nature of a sale. If you don't want to come across as obnoxious, then don't be obnoxious. You can have a convincing selling technique without being overbearing and insufferable. Second, accept that rejection is part of the package. Not everyone is going to jump at what you're offering. Focus on the ones who do. You can't allow fear of rejection to overrule success. Third, it's not egocentric to promote yourself or your product. Braggarts tend to boast about things that aren't actually true. If you have something to sell that you believe in, let people know about it. I say, if you have something worth talking about, brag away. I constantly send out information about my workshops. I truly believe they are among the best in the nation. Therefore, I feel I'm doing people a favor to let them know about it.

Second Crack: Loving What You Do

Famous late-night talk show host Johnny Carson, once said, "Never continue in a job you don't enjoy. If you're happy in what you're doing, you'll like yourself, you'll have inner peace. And if you have that, along with physical health, you will have had more success than you could possibly have imagined."

Sometimes it takes courage to do what you love.

In my workshops, I talk about the importance of doing something that you enjoy. Many people think that's impossible. The idea of work and fun in the same sentence is incomprehensible to them. But I think you'd be hard pressed to find a self-made millionaire who made their fortune doing something they despised. If you're having a hard time believing people can make millions doing something they enjoy, read "The Story of an Average Joe." I tell how found a niche that's given me the reward of loving what I do. And you can too.

Third Crack: Taking Advantage of Opportunity

Josh Billings, an American humorist, once said, "Opportunities are rare; and those who know how to seize upon them are rarer." I think that quote is absolutely true. There is opportunity all around you; you just have to open yourself up to it.

This can be difficult. Everyday life has a tendency to cloud your vision and stunt your growth. If you're just trying to survive until your next paycheck, it's hard to see opportunities. The mediocrity of life stalls dreams, and opportunities fall through the cracks.

I knew a woman who wanted to find in-home childcare for her kids, so she and her husband could work on business ideas together. Unfortunately, the nannies and au pairs the agencies sent were lackluster at best. Her husband dared her to create something better. She took him up on the dare and started a nanny and au pair agency in her basement. Within a year her agency was one of the top in the nation. She found a niche, breathed life into it, which in turn breathed life into her bank account.

As the marketing genius, Dan Kennedy says, "There are riches in niches!"

I believe everyone has at least one marketable idea that could yield a million dollars. Unfortunately, most people won't do anything to pursue it. Why? Are they afraid it won't work? Do they shy away from hard work? Or do they lack the business sense to do anything about it?

An opportunity can come from your own dissatisfaction, or by watching the ebb and flow of public demand. You may be sitting on an idea right now, afraid to let it hatch. I encourage you to hatch it, then watch it fly. You may be surprised that people have been waiting for you to pull the next best thing out of your hat.

Fourth Crack: It Pays to Be Different

Standing out in a crowd isn't always a bad thing. We're not in Junior High anymore, when blending in was the key to survival. The real world doesn't care about "blenders" – the wallflowers who blend into their surroundings so well that they're never asked to dance. The world likes color, it likes pizzazz, and it adores the daring. Be different. Feel good about yourself. Don't be afraid to show the world what you have to offer. It's the people with personality, flare and an inner light that can't get a breath because they have so many dance partners.

My advice: put on your Millionaire Shoes and get out on that dance floor!

The Story of an Average Joe

I'M LIVING PROOF that a seemingly "Average Joe" can become a millionaire. And in my case, several times over. In Step Three I talked about failing with grace—how you can't let failure lick you. You may have read that step with a bit of cynicism, thinking what does a millionaire like Lee know about failure and loss?

Actually, quite a lot.

Growing up, my family was never what you could consider rich. Yet, I would go the rounds with anyone who says you can't have a great childhood unless your family is wealthy. Even though we didn't have much money, we were, and remain to this day, a close, happy family. And money isn't required to have a good marriage either, but it helps. As Henry Ford said, "I've been poor and I've been rich. I prefer rich." I'm pretty sure his wife agreed.

Watching someone I love struggle with financial uncertainty, lead me on my path to financial success.

My father graduated from the University of Washington with a business degree. When I was in the fifth grade, he left his job in Human Resources. A few years before he had been in his prime, making good money, only six months from retirement. His working environment was stressful. The stress was mounting and he internalized it, as if it was directed at him, personally. A visit to his doctor revealed an underlying heart problem and the recommendation that he quit his job to avoid a heart attack caused by the job-related stress.

My dad decided his family would be better off with a father, but no income, than an income, but no father. So he quit, thinking he could easily find another job. But that wasn't the case. I remember mornings before school, seeing him, red-eyed and tousle-haired, half-heartedly eating cereal. He looked so broken. He had worked hard, got an education, and then found a good job. He did everything conventional wisdom told him to do. Yet, he found himself in this unfortunate situation. His downward spiral was deeper and lasted longer because he was convinced he had failed his family. And he believed he was a failure.

In the face of that, my mother took a job making only five dollars an hour to support a family of five. My father was unemployed more than a year. Then, when he did find a job, it was an entry-level position that did not utilize his degree at all.

As painful as it was, I believe this experience turned to my benefit. I realized that I held the health of my wealth in my own hands. I decided I wasn't going to let anyone but me control my financial destiny. I didn't ever want to be in the position of having to choose between working or dying.

So I became a risk taker.

I saw a nine-to-five job as more risky than starting my own business. I wanted to know that when I walked into my office, no one could hand me a pink slip and show me the door.

I didn't need a college degree to make that crystal clear. In my second year of college, I picked up the book, Rich Dad, Poor Dad by Robert Kiosaki. Something he said really stuck with me. "If you want to be rich, you need to be around rich, successful people." The idea being that you'll learn from them, their experiences and personality traits.

While sitting in my philosophy class, the significance of that notion hit me. My professor let slip that he was only making $45,000.00 a year. I dropped out of college that day. Not because I didn't respect my teacher, but because I wanted to make more than $45,000.00 a year—way more.

In Search of a Millionaire Watering Hole

After leaving college, I decided life would be my university.

Since no one actually taught me how to use money properly, I thought it was something to be used for immediate pleasure in the form of things. As a result, I made stupid purchases and damaged my credit. However, money was not to blame.

After I left college, I did my best to follow Mr. Kiosaki's advice. He said I had to run with millionaires if I wanted to find a million-dollar opportunity, and to learn their secrets to success. My personal philosophy became: no matter the social situation, I would be the poorest, dumbest person in the room. Meaning, with this attitude, I could learn from everyone there. And I decided once I joined the millionaire's circle, then I would start befriending billionaires.

The only problem was, my social group left much to be desired in the money department. I had to broaden my horizons. If I wanted to rub elbows with millionaires and billionaires, I had to find their watering holes.

Working three to midnight at a grocery store, the only free time I had was late at night. So, I looked where any smart person in my situation would look for millionaire watering holes—late night infomercials.

I could buy Ginsu knives and become a cook, buy a Chia-pet and become a gardener. Or I could go to a real estate seminar and become a real estate investor. Given the choices, only real estate held any promise of rubbing elbows with millionaires and finding my million-dollar opportunity.

The real estate infomercial company was holding a seminar in the area. It cost $1,590.00, which I didn't have. So I wrote a rubber check, then re-financed my truck to cover the check. But I went!

After the seminar, I called the real estate infomercial company to ask for a job as a speaker. I thought if I could travel the country, I could meet millionaires and find million-dollar opportunities. But the seminar company was not interested in hiring me. The prerequisite, which it seemed they were making up in an effort to discourage me, was having at least two years of sales experience, and at least ten successful real estate transactions under my belt to even be considered. I was sorely lacking in both.

The guy was just looking for a way to get rid of me, but without realizing it, he was giving me the next step on my millionaire journey. Although it was a downer, it gave me a road map to follow. I had to get started in real estate and I had to learn to sell.

Starting a real estate business required me to rethink what money was for and fix my credit rating. Had my credit been better I could have been a millionaire much sooner. After weeks of interviewing for sales positions, I finally found one at a car dealership selling used cars. Fortunately, on my first day as a "used car salesman," a packaging company I had previously interviewed with, hired me as the regional sales manager for five Pacific Northwest states. Not my dream job, but a necessary part of the journey toward my dream job. I spent the next forty-nine weeks on the road, Monday thru Friday, learning the art of sales. In the meantime I bought and sold real estate with a partner in Spokane, Washington.

On the anniversary of the second year of my journey to success, I called the real estate seminar company to tell them I had completed their prerequisites. After an interview, they hired me. I packed up and headed for their headquarters in Cape Coral, Florida, entrusting the Spokane real estate business to my partner.

Once I got to Florida, I found out the seminar company had no intention of hiring me as a speaker. They hired me for an entry-level job as part of the road crew and back of the room sales. I went from making $60,000.00 a year at the packing company, to $20,000.00 at the seminar company.

I spent the next twelve months in a weekly ritual, flying from one end of the country to the other, virtually living out of a suitcase. As part of the road crew, I sat in the back of the room, dreaming of being a speaker and reading Public Speaking for Dummies. While the position didn't pay well in dollars and cents, it was rich in experience, connections and information. I realized that many of the people who were teaching real estate courses didn't know a lot about real estate. They hadn't actually handled the nitty-gritty side of the business.

Another wrinkle was that since I was in Florida, my Spokane partner decided he didn't need to pay me my half of the rent from our rental properties. Unfortunately, the only contract I had with him was verbal, so I had no legal recourse. All in all, though it was a rough time, it was also rewarding. I gleaned an enormous amount of knowledge about the world of real estate and about life.

Pick Yourself Up, Dust Yourself Off, and Try All Over Again

It's funny how life's twists and turns can take you where you're supposed to be. While at a workshop in Salt Lake City, Utah, I noticed a pretty girl in the audience. After the seminar, Jaclyn and I exchanged phone numbers. Within six months, I made a lateral change at the seminar company and took a position as a phone consultant to be closer to her. Jumping ahead in the story, two years later, I made Jaclyn my wife.

Back to the time-line—I packed up the few belongings I hadn't already sold and moved to Utah.

By the time I got there, I was dirt poor. I had no money and nowhere to live. Jaclyn's parents kindly offered to let me stay with them until I found an apartment. And I had to borrow money from my parents to make the payments on my truck, which by then, were several months in default.

As a phone consultant, I was made even less money than I did as part of the road crew. My first paycheck was for a whopping $38.00.

I might have been broke, but I wasn't broken. I told myself over and over that one day I would be a millionaire. Believing this kept me going. I decided to do what I knew best—buying and selling real estate. The problem was, I had no money, no credit, no job, nothing. But I did have guts. I had a vision, a will and a voice. Therefore, I knew there was a way. So, I did what no sane person in that situation would do. I made an offer on a house. I offered $45,000.00 below the asking price. To my surprise, the sellers took it.

A realtor I was working with connected me with a hard-money lender. He funded the loan at an outrageous interest rate, and I bought the house. It was then that I felt the first surges of my new mantra—courage = success.

Since then, I've been involved in thousands of successful real estate transactions. And though the seminar company never did hire me as a speaker, I started my own real estate training company. Now I travel all over the country speaking and training people to use my repeatable formula for success in real estate investment.

I took many risks on my road to success. Some may see my choices as reckless and foolhardy.

I went to a real estate seminar I couldn't afford. I moved across the country and took a job with a salary a third less than I had been promised. I left my real estate business with an incompetent crook. I moved to Utah penniless and without prospects. And I took a loan from a ruthless lender.

I was able to do it by keeping my goal of future success in mind. I never doubted my ability to make millions. It culminated in meeting my beautiful wife and having a family, owning a 1.3 million dollar home, and starting my own real estate and seminar business. For me, the end has justified the means.

I went from sleeping on my future in-laws' couch to providing a beautiful home for my wife and children. I went from taking handouts from my girlfriend to pay for gas, to owning a Cadillac Escalade, a Range Rover, a Lexus, an Acura, and most recently a 4-door black Jeep Sahara that I take rock crawling in Moab, Utah.

When I set my mind to something, I know without a shadow of doubt, it will work and I will make money at it. Does that mean that I make money every time I start a new company or buy a new piece of real estate? Absolutely not, that would make me superhuman. But the old saying, "No guts, no glory," is true. It has been one of my life principles. Every move I made involved courage, risk, and in the end, results. What I focused on expanded. I found love, wealth, and happiness because I knew I would and I believe you can too.

Investing in Real Estate

Since I made my millions in real estate, readers have asked about my real estate investment principles. I've included a simplified version of some points I cover in my seminars—what I look for in investment properties.

Motivated Sellers – This category includes people who are about to lose their property to foreclosure. It includes those going through a death in the family or divorce. It could also include people who changed jobs and are making two or three mortgage payments. If there is a reason the property is hurting the seller's financial bottom line, then chances are you can make a profit on it.

Distressed Properties – Most distressed properties aren't in nearly as bad condition as people think. A coat of paint, new carpet, a few upgrades, and these properties typically make a nice investment.

Highest and Best Use – It's nothing more than creating a different use for a piece of ground, than what it's currently used for. A common example is converting an apartment building into condominiums. Or converting farmland into building lots. Highest and best use is my favorite real estate investment technique. Thinking outside the box creates value where no one saw potential.

I've fine-tuned my workshops to be more productive and user-friendly than the other seminars out there. I want my participants to leave with the nuts and bolts of real estate investing. I want them to graduate knowing how to make a living at real estate. And I will mentor them on their road to wealth.

When you finish this book, call my office and ask how my five-year $100,000,000.00 goal is going. Or, catch me at one of my seminars. You can use the coupon in the front of the book for a $500.00 discount. Then corner me and ask how I'm progressing on my goal. I'd love to tell you about it.

CONCLUSION

Walk the Walk of a Millionaire

All our dreams can come true, if we have the courage to pursue them. - Walt Disney -

I see my path, but I don't know where it leads. Not knowing where I'm going is what inspires me to travel it. - Rosalia de Castro -

Joining the Mighty Few

You are at a crossroads.

You can either close this book and continue on your current path, or you can venture off into a new world of wealth, success and a life worth living. Truly the three are interrelated. You've already taken the first steps to wearing your Millionaire Shoes. If you've done the exercises, you know that your mind-set brought you to this point.

You are at the crossroads. Which direction will you go?

ON THE ROAD TO RICHES

The best day of your life is the one on which you decide your life is your own. No apologies or excuses. No one to lean on, rely on, or to blame. The gift is yours - it is an amazing journey - and you alone are responsible for the quality of it. This is the day your life really begins.

~ Bob Moawad
Chairman and CEO of
Edge Learning Institute

The next step is to close your eyes and jump. Yes, you read it correctly, jump. Take a deep breath, close your eyes, and take the plunge. I know some of you are shaking your head in disbelief. But like rock climbing, parachuting, or even jumping off the high dive, it's all about getting over your fear. The rest is simply gravity. After that first jump everything else seems easy.

That next step is all about trusting yourself. It takes courage and faith in your ability, and following the steps in this book to join the ranks of those who wear Millionaire Shoes.

It begins by having the courage to put them on.

Some of you will try them on, then take them off. Some will wear them a little longer. But some will put them on, decide to live in them and never take them off. To those of you who are determined to wear your Millionaire Shoes, I say, "Go for it!"

I have yet to meet a successful person who, after making his or her first million, looks back on the journey and says, "Gee, I learned a lot, and I was successful, but I don't want to do that again."

It takes a special person to live in Millionaire Shoes. The great thing is: anyone can become that special kind of person. They are like you and me. They're not genetically predisposed to being wealthy. They haven't benefited from "survival of the fittest" evolutionary traits that allow them to succeed where others have failed. They're not superhuman, just super-successful. The good news is that super-successfulness can be learned.

To re-cap: it's a process of reinvention. It begins with a dream, which morphs into an action, which becomes the realization. You obviously have the inclination; or you wouldn't have finished this book. That's how it starts. A wistful idea turns into a full-fledged goal. This book, and books like it, will help you get from the dream to the reality.

Finding a Money Mentor

men·tor [men-tawr, -ter] 1. Someone whose hindsight can become your foresight.

Travel only with thy equals or thy betters; if there are none, travel alone. - The Dhammapada -

You don't have to walk in your Millionaire Shoes all alone. As with any training program, having an encouraging teacher and friend makes the challenge easier. Having someone there to give you a push when you begin to waver, makes the night-and-day difference for many people.

Most self-made millionaires have mentors, who are also self-made millionaires. See how it works? To become a millionaire, you have to act like one. To act like one, you'll have to get to know one or two. Most, most self-made millionaires are just like you, except they have more money.

How do you find your money mentor?

Once you find the niche where you want to make your millions, look for someone who has already done it in that field. Attend their workshops if they have them, work for their company, or become an apprentice. Their hindsight can be your foresight.

You may be thinking, "Yeah right, like it's that easy." You never know unless you try. Remember, no guts, no glory. Take my story. I made many mistakes on my road to wealth that you don't have to make. And you can learn from my successes.

Start by reading and rereading books like this one. There are lots of financial wizards out there who have put their secrets on paper. They spell out answers to the riddles that have kept you in the red and teach you how to live in the black. I read and re-read empowering books by encouraging authors.

Authors like:

- Dan Kennedy, author of *The Ultimate Secret to Success.*
- Dan Airely, author of *Predictably Irrational: The Hidden Forces That Shape Our Decisions.*
- Robert G. Allen, author of *Nothing Down and Creating Wealth.*
- Thomas J. Stanley Ph.D., author of *The Millionaire Next Door.*
- Napoleon Hill, author of *Think and Grow Rich*
- Dale Carnegie, author of *How to Win Friends and Influence People*
- Suze Orman, author of *The 9 Steps to Financial Freedom.*

- Mark Victor Hansen, author of *Chicken Soup for the Soul.*
- And God, author of *The Holy Bible.* Proverbs is probably the best financial book ever written

Finding a millionaire mentor is one step. On the flip side, severing ties with people who try to hold you down is another. Misery loves company and a miserable person never wants to hear success stories. They are happier hearing about your failures. Pressure to keep you from your millions will always be present. Overcoming it can mean letting go of friends and family who try to discourage you from wearing your Millionaire Shoes.

The Victory Lap

> *Victory is won not in miles but in inches. Win a little now, hold your ground, and later, win a little more. - Louis L'Amour -*

Once you've earned your first million you can take a victory lap. You can even take two, if you want.

When you overcome poverty, you can become the epitome of plenty.

The process of reinventing yourself isn't easy. Earning the first million takes a lot of blood, sweat and tears. You're reprogramming the way you think, feel and act. It's not just about making money, it's also about living a more fulfilling life. Each step you take forward is a step toward that better life financially, mentally, and emotionally.

By honing your financial skills, you can travel the road to riches over and over again. And each time it will be a little easier.

Happy Trails to You

The fool wanders, a wise man travels.
- Thomas Fuller -

Often, the human mind-set is to analyze rather than act. To want rather than have. To hesitate rather than go forward full throttle. To play for time rather than play to win.

By and large we're a cautionary society. We tiptoe instead of walking with purpose. I encourage you to stop dillydallying. If you want to walk in Millionaire Shoes, you'll have to go into action. You can't simply dream yourself into millions. Although it's the first step, it's by no means the last.

This reminds me of a humorous story.

The novelist Sinclair Lewis was supposed to deliver an hour-long lecture to a group of college students who planned to be writers. Lewis opened his talk with a question:

"How many of you really intend to be writers?"

All hands went up.

"In that case," said Lewis, "my advice to you is to go home and write."

And with that, he left.

You can read book after financial book, and attend lecture after lecture, and invest in multiple "Get Rich Quick Schemes," but nothing will come of any of it without focused action. Remember, nothing comes from nothing. If you want to wear Millionaire Shoes, you'll have to put in million-dollar effort.

Decide to do it today.

There is no need to wander anymore. Everything you need is at your fingertips. All you have to do is take these steps outlined here to heart and put them into action. I can give you the advice in this book and I can offer you a spot at one of my workshops, but then it's up to you. You either make the decision to put one foot in front of the other, or you stick this book on a shelf somewhere and walk away. My hope is that you put on your Millionaire Shoes and start walking.

I'll be rooting for you. I want to share the wealth.

From my family to yours, may God truly bless and enrich you.

If a goal is not written down, it's only a wish.

To print the check on the following page:

Go to **www.theleearnoldsystem.com/shoes** and print your copy seen onsceen at the mentioned website.

1. Put your name, the amount you wish to receive, and the date you want to receive it by on your Goal Motivating check.

2. Place your check in a prominent place where you will see it every day. Do not take it down until the date or goal has been realized.

3. Every time you look at your check, visualize, believe and feel that you have the money now!

Print out the check, fill in your name and the amount you wish to receive.

I KNOW I WILL DO IT

DOMINATING THOUGHTS BANK UNLIMITED

Your dominating thought is your future reality

LeeArnold SYSTEM OF REAL ESTATE INVESTING

REMITTANCE ADVICE—*Be Positive*

Date:___/___/___

PAY ________________________ **$** ________

TO THE AMOUNT OF ________________________ **DOLLARS**

This is not an instrument subject to article 3 of the UCC

By signing, I guarantee I will achieve this goal!

⑆1234267891⑆1234267891⑈

WWW.THELEEARNOLDSYSTEM.COM

ABOUT THE AUTHOR

Lee A. Arnold is the CEO of Secured Investment Corp, Private Money Exchange and a new and rapidly growing brick and mortar private money lending company called Cogo Captial™ "The Private Money Company"™.

He grew up in a traditional American family where a college education was taught as the only way to reach financial security. Yet, when his own highly educated father faced a career loss, his family went through a long period of living in financial strain. Lee knew from that moment on he never wanted his income or his future to be left in the hands of someone else.

Lee's desire to reach the heights of financial freedom has allowed him to discover unique investing methods and innovative strategies that many other real estate investors have no idea about. Through hard work, in-depth research, and years of full time investing, Lee truly has found the golden key to unlock the door to financial success.

Lee has generated millions of dollars in personal wealth and is known as one of the foremost experts in the foreclosure and short sale industry. His goal is to help other investors discover the same success he has found and experience the joy of a truly rewarding career.

If you would like to contact Lee call us at 1-800-558-6092. We look forward to your call!

Or visit: www.theleearnoldsystem.com